THE STORY OF
ATKINSONS

By Neil Anderson

Published by ACM Retro Ltd,
Registered office:
51 Clarkegrove Road,
Sheffield,
S10 2NH.

Visit ACM Retro at:
www.acmretro.com

Neil Anderson asserts the moral right to be identified as the author of this work.

A catalogue record for this book is available from the British Library.

CONTENTS

The first purpose-built Atkinsons department store is decked out for the Easter Fayre in the 1920s.

FOREWORD
by Nicholas Atkinson - great grandson of the founder, John Atkinson

It gives me great pleasure to introduce this book on the history of Atkinsons.

A few years ago this might have been written about one of the other great independent retail institutions built in our great city over the decades like Walsh's or Cockaynes. They, like us, survived the Sheffield Blitz but today, Atkinsons are the one surviving independent department store left in Sheffield.

We believe it's our history that has seen us through, a history that is about to embark on another exciting chapter in our long life.

When my great grandfather, John Atkinson, opened his small drapery shop on The Moor in 1872, it was always his policy to offer his customers, quality, value and service. He knew that if he was to get customers to return to his shop, time and time again, this was the approach to have.

Quality, value and service were implicit in his successful business and that same ethos runs through the business today.

Atkinsons customers know that we will always look after them and that is why we have such a strong and loyal customer base today. They value our emphasis on service and trust that is so often lacking in many other businesses.

Over the years we have seen generations of families shopping with us. Talking and interacting with our customers is an important part of keeping in touch with families and ensuring they want to continue shopping with us in the future.

From the start, the business has always adapted to change. At the turn of the century (1900) the store that was on the site of our present store was way ahead of its time. It was the first department store to build a large atrium in the roof which let natural light flood down through a stairwell, lighting up all the floors, so that customers could see the real colour of garments.

Then again in 1960 when the present store opened, replacing the old store which had been burnt to the ground during the Blitz in 1940, Atkinsons was the first store in Sheffield to introduce 'self service' selling, where customer helped themselves and took goods to a cash point, rather than being served behind a counter.

In the mid-1990s The Moor area became more neglected. This was due to two main issues, the development of Meadowhall and the handing over of the entire Moor area to private developers.

Meadowhall took the cream of retailing out of the city centre and the private developers took fifteen years to decide what was to happen to The Moor. In the meantime shops on the precinct fell into disrepair and it has only been since Scottish Widows Investment Properties has taken the area over in the last few years that matters have at last taken a very positive turn, with the centre of Sheffield returning to The Moor and major retailers now returning. The future is indeed brighter.

A few years ago everyone was talking about 'The cloned High Street'. The view was that every High Street / Shopping Centre had the same mix and shopping was becoming very repetitive and that new life should be bred into the retail mix.

As an independent department store covering 75,000 sq ft of selling space, with 36 departments, four restaurants, its own car park for 440 cars above the store and a buying team of 10, we firmly believe we are very different to what is found on the High Street . Add to that our personal service and value, puts us well on a par with the competition.

The people of Sheffield will always want to shop in 'the High Street' shop at some time. People love the interactivity of retail therapy and to be able to talk and relax with friends in a pleasant environment. Atkinsons has it all.

CHAPTER ONE
The beginnings

The Sheffield town of 1865 that first welcomed John Atkinson must have been a sombre place in many quarters.

Just a few months prior, in 1864, it had been the setting for the catastrophic Great Sheffield Flood. Hundreds of people lost their lives as millions of gallons of water came crashing down the valley from the nearby Dale Dyke Reservoir.

It swept down the course of the River Loxley to Hillsborough, and then down the Don and on through the town itself.

In some cases the wall of water reached thirty feet high. Homes, farmhouses and every manner of dwelling were crushed in its wake.

Many people were drowned in their sleep as the dam burst in the dead of night in a bitterly cold March.

Even in the Wicker, within a quarter of a mile of where the first Atkinsons store would open a few years later, the wall of water was sufficiently high to run over the parapet of Lady's Bridge and flood streets and houses to a depth of five feet.

The Great Sheffield Flood ended up killing 238 people, 700 livestock and destroyed or damaged over 600 properties.

The disaster changed the town of Sheffield forever.

A relief effort called on anyone who could afford it to give up a day's pay to help the homeless and needy. Souvenirs were produced to mark the tragedy and raise money for victims.

Maybe it took the arrival of newcomers like John Atkinson and their entrepreneurial ideas to give the town something new and positive to focus upon.

He was one of nine siblings that originally lived in Low Dunsforth, near Boroughbridge.

John Atkinson believed he had a head for business from an early age.

Many sleepless nights ensued as the young man debated on where best to advance his career.

The first place to tempt him was the City of York with its imposing walls.

John Atkinson witnessed the excitement around the newly formed North Eastern Railway Company and the proliferation of the iron network spreading across the country. He stayed in employment in York for five years but ambition couldn't contain him - a thirst for an endeavour of his own consumed him.

Sheffield was already well known to him. It supplied the trains with their rails. 'Made In Sheffield' was the mark that appeared on cutlery and plate around the world. It was a global industrial powerhouse.

Other centres had challenged Steel City for the crown but they'd failed. John Atkinson realised it was a town with a future and he hoped he could be a major part of it. But he didn't realise his ambition straight away - far from it in fact.

Historian W. W. Chisholm said in 1922: "John Atkinson's first transaction with the Sheffield shopping public was as a humble shop assistant of Cole Brothers, in their premises at the corner of Church Street ."

His next move, in 1870, was the start of his rise to retail icon and the first time the name 'Atkinson' appeared on the streets of the town. But at this point he wasn't going it alone as he only owned fifty percent of the business.

King & Atkinson drapers opened up at 81, West Street. But it wasn't to last. He soon realised the only way he was going to find true success was to have a totally free hand in business.

Sheffield - a town of prosperity

He wasn't alone in thinking Sheffield was a place he could do business. The town - in the lead up to the flood - was a gathering hotbed of industrial and cultural might and news of its success was spreading.

The town was already on a high following the publication of the groundbreaking 'Illustrated Guide to Sheffield' - the 1862 book many cite as the future city's first serious foray into tourism

The title gives an interesting insight into the kinds of retail competition faced by John Atkinson in Sheffield.

There was R. & G. Gray & Co. drapers in Fargate's Victoria Buildings selling everything from 'baby linen' to 'German, Swiss & Nottingham curtains'.

They offered 'Berlin Wool' (the country was still decades

off World War One and an anti-German backlash), 'Paris and London Millinery Bonnets' and all manner of fancy goods.

R. & G. Gray & Co. were geared up to serve the upper echelons of Victorian Sheffield and they'd bought a two page advert in the guide book to help market their wares. The majority of adverts in the book were taken up by long gone steel giants but look closer and you see other familiar names like George Bassett confectioners that have stood the test of time.

There was no getting away from the grime and smoke that existed in a town that was at the forefront of the industrial revolution but, as is still the case today, it was its green surroundings that were seen as the icing on the cake.

As the book states: "Although Sheffield is of course in its manufacturing parts not more clean or less smoky than other similar centres of industry, there is perhaps no large town in the kingdom situated in the midst of so charming and picturesque a district."

Moor life before Atkinsons

In the late 1860s and early 1870s the top of The Moor area was viewed as containing some of the least desirable shops and dwellings anywhere in the town. They were described as "relics of a forgotten age". On one side you'd got Backfields, formerly a rural street approaching Barker's Pool. Nearby you'd got shops of all description running up the old wall of St Pauls (the church later demolished to make way for the modern day Peace Gardens).

The area was intertwined with narrow cart tracks and primitively constructed buildings.

Sport was one of the main pastimes of the age and one of the main attractions was Bramall Lane which was a few minutes' walk from The Moor (which was then called South Street, Sheffield Moor). Cricket and football were the mainstay of the ground.

It was the period that started to see the area becoming one of the busiest retail areas of the town. One drawback was cited - the lack of entertainment opportunities.

There were no variety halls, amateur operatic bodies or anything else. Things on offer were generally more lowbrow than highbrow. Public houses serving until 1am, visiting circuses and 'rat-pits' where enormous crowds paid to witness terrier dogs killing as many rodents in a minute as possible.

The wider Sheffield town of this time couldn't be more different than it is today.

W. W. Chisholm said: "Fulwood Road was a lovely country lane where beautiful wild flowers bloomed in summer, on the lower ground the River Porter babbled as it ran through Whiteley Woods and Endcliffe...

"The Park district was amongst the most interesting. Hyde Park was not comparable with Norfolk Park, but it had attractions and afforded a charming view."

William Ibbitt, an old-time artist of repute, painted a picture from this spot which pointed to the fact you could stand near Hyde Park and see the time on the Rotherham Church clock!

It wouldn't be long before the smoke of industry would put paid to any chance of that...

Top of The Moor in 1863

CHAPTER TWO

John Atkinson arrives on South Street, Sheffield Moor

Success comes to those who wait...
It's a phrase that could have been written for John Atkinson. After his years of being the apprentice boy in York, his time as a Cole Bros shop assistant and his two years in the 'King and Atkinson' partnership on West Street, fate had finally come knocking at his door.

He was offered premises in South Street, Sheffield Moor.

The move was a step too far for King and the business relationship was dissolved amicably.

For John Atkinson it was the perfect outcome: he finally had the freedom, the premises and, thanks to his earlier West Street business, the experience to start realising his dream.

No. 90, South Street, Sheffield Moor, was an unpretentious, two-windowed shop. But for John Atkinson it was a dream come true. It was finally down to him to make a go of things.

When the shutters came up on the spring morning of 1872, the Atkinson story had truly begun.

John Atkinson might have been just 26 years old with hardly any working capital but, what he lacked in cash and maturity, he made up for with entrepreneurial drive.

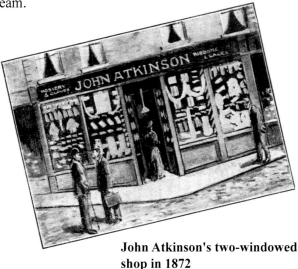

John Atkinson's two-windowed shop in 1872

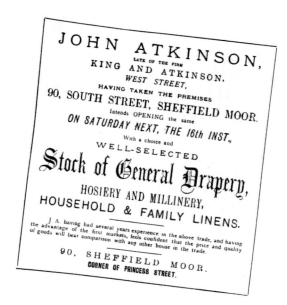

Advert announcing John Atkinson's arrival on The Moor

If youthful bravado did ever get the better of him and he thought about boasting of his achievements thus far he was about to be introduced to the biggest reality check of his life.

The hours of self sacrifice required to hone the business in the early years were unrelenting and would have probably broken lesser men.

But never in his wildest dreams could he ever have imagined the legacy he was about to unleash.

One that has gone on to serve generations of Sheffielders for over 140 years; provide jobs for thousands of people and survived being flattened in the Blitz to become one of the most revered family owned department stores in the county.

John Atkinson specialised in hosiery, ribbons and lace. It wasn't anything that couldn't be bought anywhere else but he hoped his boundless enthusiasm and dedication to his work would win business and support from the locals.

Quality merchandise, value for money prices and exemplary customer service were his ideals - ideals that are as important today as they were in 1872.

Ideals of another kind were being introduced to the citizens of Sheffield that year. Public houses were required to have licences and drinking hours were cut - to the displeasure of more than a few.

It was also the year of the very first FA Cup. Though Sheffield was already boasting the world's oldest club in the shape of Sheffield FC (formed in 1857), the town wasn't represented.

The silverware was battled out between Wanderers and Royal Engineers on 16 March at Kennington Oval in London.

The British Empire was still in expansion mode on the global front whilst Thomas Edison was nearing the launch of an early light bulb and phonograph.

It would be four years after John Atkinson first opened that Alexander Graham Bell would be parading his prototype telephone.

South Street payback

Seven years of long hours and hard work followed before John Atkinson's dedication started to really show signs of paying off.

Indeed E. E. Chisholm, referring to the period fifty years later, said: "They were years in which the head of the house knew little of relaxation, years in which incessant toil, assiduous attention to every branch of business, and consistency of purpose bore fruit...

"But the growing assurance that the customer's interests were as fully considered as were those of the trader, slowly and surely won the trust and confidence of a steadily growing volume of regular customers. And the walls seemed to grow closer together. Elbow room was lacking. Assistants in the morning were almost buried by the goods they sold by nightfall, and customers crowded upon each other from morning to night."

It's fair to say fortune must have been shining on John Atkinson - the severity and length of the British depression of 1875 to 1878 is regularly compared to the one we're experiencing in the UK today, one that has in recent years put scores of household retail names out of business. Amazingly, it hardly affected the business.

Maybe it's not surprising Atkinsons are the only surviving independent department store in Sheffield, no one else has had as much practice of dealing with the ups and downs of the British economy!

John Atkinson's former employer - Cole Bros store on the corner of Church Street

CHAPTER THREE
The great Victorian expansion

There's more than a few key dates in the rich tapestry that is the Atkinsons story but, as far as the Victorian period was concerned, 1879 was the year of the major step forward and the first sign that John Atkinson was truly a name to watch in business.

The man that started it all, John Atkinson

It was the first time that the word 'expansion' was uttered - a word that, generations later, seems almost second nature to a company that knows investment is the key to future prosperity.

Sheffield town was developing in leaps and bounds at the time.

Notable attractions like Weston Park Museum (complete with its star attractions, the Egyptian mummies); Bramall Lane Cricket Ground (it didn't become SUFC's home until a decade later); Glossop Road baths; Firth College (now the Leopold Hotel following many years as Sheffield Central Technical School) and the Hallamshire Savings Bank on Norfolk Street (now a public house) have all stood the test of time and remain to this day.

Day outs visiting Chatsworth, Haddon Hall, Hathersage or Castleton were very much in vogue - a popular pastime that hasn't really changed.

The town's population was around 200,000.It would be starting to nudge its present day level of 500,000 by the outbreak of World War One - just four decades later - as thousands poured into Sheffield to work in the expanding steel trade.

Many locals would have been keeping a close eye on happenings overseas in 1879, 150 soldiers had defended the Rorke's Drift supply station against 4,000 Zulu warriors in January of that year.

There'd probably be no better place to read and discuss the progress of the war than the upmarket Sheffield Club on Norfolk Street.

Described as "similar to the Clubs of London", it opened in 1862.

It makes you wonder if John Atkinson toasted his success in there in 1879 - the year he extended his South Street, Sheffield Moor, interests into the two adjoining premises - number 86 and 88.

His existing business was literally bursting at the seams and it was fair to say Sheffielders had truly taken him and his business principles to their hearts.

Mrs Elizabeth Atkinson nee Eshelby, John's mother

John Atkinson moved into number 88 and let out number 86 to a fellow trader.

The growth of the business was very much in line with growing confidence within the city and country at the time.

E.E. Chisholm said of the period: "Space and still more space was indispensible, and so, after suffering the growing inconvenience of being cabined and confined until 1884, No. 86 was taken in hand and fitted out as a millinery department."

It's fair to say it was the year John Atkinson was truly starting to exude confidence. He was also proving he had a very good measure of people - vital in any retail business.

E. E. Chisholm said of the year: "Mr. Atkinson was finding growing pleasure in his business, for his business was truly his pleasure. There was almost hydraulic pressure in the measure of his business. "Happily the chief was a man who had a great knowledge of character. He knew the man or the woman whom he could trust to conduct certain branches of his lines; but, at the same time, whilst he used the services of these estimable helpers, he knew the falsity of the old proverb about having too many irons in the fire, and continued to have every implement therein, and, moreover, kept them very hot."

Three years later and expansion was back at the top of the agenda once more. Nos. 2, 4 and 6 of the adjacent Prince Street were added. John Atkinson needed them to develop his new furniture trade. Business was truly booming.

But there was one thing that was increasingly worrying him - the overall appearance of his growing collection of premises.

This was a man who spent time working in the beautiful City of York, he'd got used to stunning architecture and wanted it for his own premises.

He was also in agreement with celebrated art critic and philanthropist John Ruskin, who was at that time devoting a lot of time to the town of Sheffield and believed a place is measured on the standard of its architecture.

John Atkinson was renowned as a man who never let his ambition cool and, in terms of aesthetics, it wouldn't be a subject that was off the agenda for long.

Four years later and his burgeoning retail empire was on the move again. This time into the extensive space at the back of Prince Street which was secured and covered for the development of the mantle and shawl trade.

Fashion was key to much of John Atkinson's business and women observed it as much in the 1880s as they do today.

He knew its secret was to surprise and never to disappoint; his latest extension was designed to offer the best and latest creations at the best possible price. It was another masterstroke.

Department after department was added and by 1892, another pivotal year in the story, John Atkinson had purchased shops, land and works that made up 76 to 86 South Street, The Moor, together with further works covering a large block of buildings as far back as nearby Button Lane, facing Eldon Street.

Five years later a new Dress Warehouse was erected in Holy Green - a stretch of land that bordered South Street, Sheffield Moor, that was in front of the residence of Thomas Holy, one of the town's most notable worthies who was renowned for entertaining John Wesley, the originator of the Methodist Church.

This was at the back of 86 and 88 South Street, Sheffield Moor, and allowed for more space for the ever-increasing demands of the dress goods and silk trade departments.

Working for Atkinsons has always been regarded as joining one big, happy family and the early days were no different. Here's a staff outing in the late 1890s

CHAPTER FOUR

The unveiling of the first purpose-built Atkinsons store

Despite his growing success, John Atkinson's love of architecture was increasingly getting the better of him.

Whilst many would have been happy with such a thriving business, the ad hoc collection of buildings that housed his burgeoning empire was becoming an incessant bugbear.

Never far from his mind was the fact he'd grown up near the splendour of nearby Ripon Cathedral and Fountains Abbey; spent his early working life in the architecture of York and he was now surrounded by the Victorian style of Sheffield city centre - prior to the Blitz of December 1940 the area boasted quite an impressive collection of enviable buildings.

In fact nothing came more awe-inspiring than Sheffield's shiny new Town Hall that was unveiled by Queen Victoria in 1896 - a structure, thankfully, largely untouched by the German bombings a few decades later.

It wasn't long after the festivities had died down from New Year's Eve of 1899 that John Atkinson made, arguably, the most far-reaching decision of his life - demolish all the shops ranging from no. 76 to 86 South Street and start again!

E. E. Chisholm said: "Necessity urged desperate measures and with the stimulant that drove to a bigger undertaking than any that had preceded it. In 1900 it was absolutely imperative in order to meet the demands of customers that the practicality of demolishing all the shops ranging from Nos. 76 to 86 on the South Street site and erecting a substantial well-

designed building in their stead should be faced."

The foundation stone for the brand new store was laid in 1901. Work started at a furious pace, so much so that the building was completed and ready for occupation the following year.

It makes you wonder if the 1901 date was a deliberate move. The 20th century started with an argument of national importance in the country because Britain couldn't quite make up its mind where one century finished and another one started.

On one side you'd got the 'zeroists' who were convinced one era stopped in 1899 and another started in 1900 whilst the majority decided 1900 was actually the last year of the last century and most people held their celebrations on the eve of 1901.

Queen Victoria died only a few days later, on January 22, 1901. She wasn't in the best of health when she visited Sheffield a few years earlier to open the Town Hall - she never actually left her carriage.

'Zeroist' or preferring to wait until the eve of 1901, there's no doubt John Atkinson's architectural dream

The new Atkinsons in 1902

was about to be realised.

The new building was stunning. It wasn't long before ground and first floor were woven into a network of departments and an army of attentive attendants ready to greet the influx of customers.

By this time he'd also been joined by his sons, Harold Atkinson (born in 1879) and Walter Atkinson (born in 1884). The building opened with great excitement in 1902.

It was a world away from the gas illuminated shop of 1872 and the business truly hit the ground running. You could hardly move for Atkinsons in the early part of the last century as the new store opened. Rival traders must have wondered what had hit them as the store attracted more and more shoppers from the Fargate area of Sheffield - home to key rivals like

Cockaynes and Walsh's - to the bottom of The Moor. Their adverts adorned trams, Sheffield directories, the pages of newspapers and they even sponsored the 'A.B.C. Guide to Electricity' which advised citizens of this exciting new invention.

In fact, Atkinsons were marketing themselves as 'The All-Electric House' at the time.

The new building and increased profile was obviously the impetus they needed.

By 1912 they were ready to expand their borders yet again; the lease for premises which had been the residence of Mr Thomas Holy came up for sale.

The historic old house, which had for many years been occupied as the Ecclesall Club, was converted into a warehouse for the business.

New arcades at 86, 88 and 90 South Street, Sheffield Moor, were opened in February of 1914. It was also a period of intense activity as much of the interior of the existing store was replanned to introduce much more clearly defined departments.

It was quite a feat of building - in just 28 days workers completely remodelled the interior with the help of tons of steel girders and hundreds of tons of bricks.

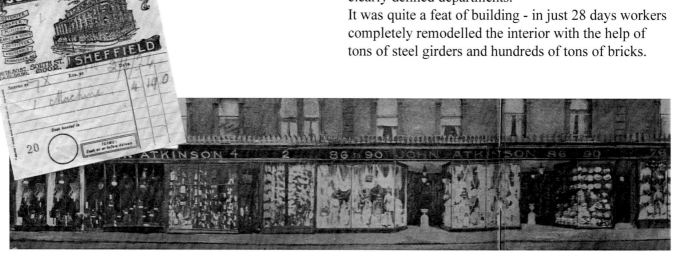

The ever expanding Atkinsons prior to demolition

A basket of strawberries for Harold Atkinson's wedding

David Owen was the store's accountant from 1898 to 1931.

His first memory of Atkinsons was his invitation to the wedding of Harold Atkinson, John Atkinson's son.

It took the shape of an outing to Monsal Dale in the company of staff. The excited party set out in four horse-drawn coaches - each one supplied with its own basket of strawberries.

David Owen's son later recalled of his father's trip and said: "On arrival at Monsal Head the party were given a meal and then returned to Sheffield via the Peacock at Owler Bar, where further refreshment was partaken. "Mr Owen well remembers coming down the hill from Owler Bar into Sheffield in the dark with the big oil lamps of the coaches shining on the backs of the horses."

Dark clouds gather

Nobody could have foreseen the carnage that was to follow the idyllic summer of 1914.
The countdown to war was the sole discussion in Atkinsons and shops across the city on Tuesday, August 4.
The declaration of war was expected that day. The news finally arrived at 11pm that evening - Britain was at war

Advert for the new store

Sheffield tram with Atkinsons advert

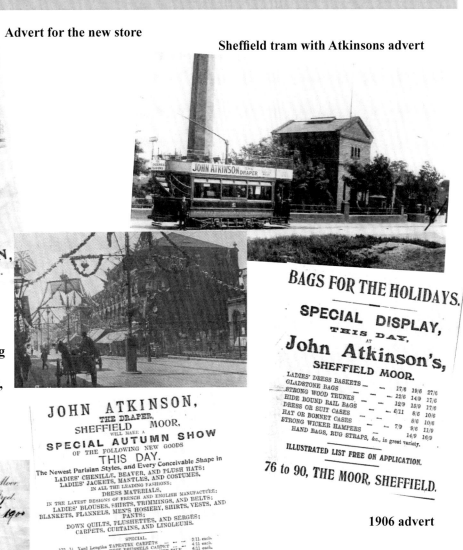

The Moor and Atkinsons in July 1905 decorated for the visit of King Edward and Queen Alexandra to officially open Sheffield University, Weston Park

Letter from John Atkinson to mark his son's 21st birthday

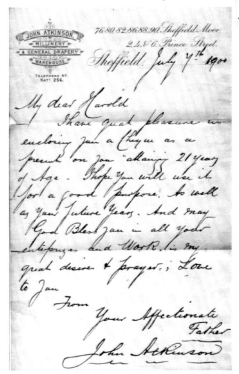

1906 advert

The Atkinsons cricket team with John Atkinson (right)

JOHN ATKINSON,

THE DRAPER.

SPRING, 1898.

New SPRING SHOW to-day in all Departments.

Millinery, Mantles, Flowers, Feathers, Capes, Furs, Jackets, Dress Materials, Silks, Velvets, Satin, Velveteens, Gloves, Umbrellas, Hosiery, Ribbons, Laces, Trimming, Buttons, &c.

Furnishing Drapery, Carpets, Linoleums, Bedsteads, Bedding, &c.

86 to 90, Sheffield Moor; Prince Street, & Eldon Street,

SHEFFIELD.

Advert for Atkinsons prior to demolition from spring 1898

CHAPTER FIVE

The Great War years

Sheffield's Armistice Day celebrations of 1918 were muted and short-lived for many. It was a hollow victory at the side of four years of slaughter on the battlefields of France and Belgium; the loss of thousands of young Sheffield lives and Germany bringing the battlefront to the civilian streets of the city in 1916 with a devastating Zeppelin raid.

Atkinsons were firmly behind the war effort

The bloodiest and most savage conflict ever undertaken by the country began on August 4, 1914. It was a date that was set to change the shape of the Atkinsons business for the duration of the war and beyond.

A tidal wave of patriotism swept the nation initially as young men from all backgrounds queued up to join Lord Kitchener's new style of army.

This wasn't the normal kind of military force, this was something untried and dreamt up by the new Secretary of State for War to swell the military ranks and satisfy the insatiable appetite of the growing battle front on the continent.

Unbelievably, the initial target of 100,000 raw recruits was met within days, and a month later over half a million men had volunteered across the country.

Enthusiasm for taking the fight to Berlin was no greater than in Atkinsons.

E. E. Chisholm said: "Men went from counter and warehouse to the trenches, and such as were left behind, old servants and indispensables, "carried on"."

A jubilant crowd gathered outside Sheffield Town Hall on the afternoon of September 2, 1914, to watch the initial wave of volunteers go inside and sign up.

The first man to complete the formalities was Vivian Sumner Simpson. He, when compared to the bulk of the men that time ran out for on July 1, 1916, at the Battle of the Somme, had a good innings - he was killed just weeks before Germany surrendered in April 1918.

The formation of the Sheffield City Battalion (or Sheffield 'PALS' as they became better known) was different to everything that had gone before as it allowed men with similar social and professional backgrounds to serve together with the aim of creating a happy atmosphere and a more efficient unit - it was a model repeated up and down the country.

Atkinsons shop workers lined up besides lawyers, journalists, students, manual labourers - there was hardly a trade not represented by the rookie soldiers who did some of their early training at Bramall Lane football and cricket ground before moving to Redmires on the outskirts of the city.

The fact no one had an ounce of military experience, a uniform or anything bar their bare hands to kill any Germans in the early months of training could not quell their eagerness to get to France and 'do their bit'.

Indeed E. E. Chisholm said the Kaiser's threat pushed

the menfolk of Sheffield over the edge. He said: "Men who had never shouldered anything more deadly than a toy rifle realised the peril and crowded the centres for recruiting, while those engaged in heavy trades and those whose occupation was in the stores were training for defence of the homeland and the protection of those whose homes in France and Flanders were being flattened and overrun.

"There was response to the call as it ran down The Moor. Every shop turned out its quota of men and youths and maidens, for those who were not accepted for the field of battle or for the ships that kept the seas for Britain were taken into shops that were asked to supply munitions of war. It was not until 1915 that this demand for help by the smaller factories was made by the Secretary of State for War. Then all firms and establishments were urged to lose no time in adapting any works, shops, etc, to the making of whatever would be serviceable as munitions or for other purposes of warfare."

The loss of a large percentage of its young male workforce wasn't the only change at Akinsons in the Great War.

Much of the premises were turned over to machine shops to produce essentials for the military campaign. E. E. Chisholm said: "It was at this critical period that the firm of John Atkinson had available a large empty area of works that had been vacated by cutlery workers and those engaged in allied trades, together with large stables and yard accommodation. Every endeavour was made to utilise the buildings and the space. Old grinding hulls were of no use, nor were the engine houses, etc. They were swept away almost as ruthlessly as were buildings in Rheims, and in their places were erected shops for drop stamping. Without any delay work began, and it continued without intermission until November, 1918."

Atkinsons threw itself into the war effort.

"From 1915 to 1918 the firm was responsible for making many hundreds of thousands of stamped parts for all descriptions of guns, shells, and tanks. The development was extensive, and the variety that was produced was surprisingly great. Stamping and drop forging produced such things as gun pivots, air vessel ends, crank-cases for aero-engines, discs, breech rings, breech screws, shell components, bolts and nuts, parts for lorries, brackets, levers, swivels, and things the name of which had never been uttered on The Moor."

Atkinsons also circulated free wool to Sheffield women who volunteered to knit hats to fit inside the tin helmets of soldiers, to make the unwieldy items more comfortable.

Even though great swathes of the business was devoted to the war effort, demands for greater space for the retail division continued.

Two new wings were added at the end of 1918.

Remembering the Sheffield City Battalion

Over 3,000 men passed through the ranks of the Sheffield City Battalion in its short life.

It was disbanded, just three and half years after it was formed, on February 28, 1918. There was little left of the once proud outfit.

Survivors returning home cut ghostly figures as they struggled to return to civilian life, few ever spoke of the horrors they'd witnessed.

The Sheffield City Battalion is forever remembered for its part in arguably the greatest military disaster in British history, the Battle of the Somme.

It was the summer's morning of July 1, 1916, when the city's young men clambered into no-man's-land and set off on their measured walk towards the German lines.

The enemy, unbeknown to them, had hardly been bothered by the hours of relentless shelling by the British leading up the attack and the German machine guns slaughtered the bulk of Sheffield City Battalion within minutes.

That day saw 548 Sheffielders killed or wounded - including men from Atkinsons. Over 50,000 men were lost by the British that day.

Novelist John Harris gave a sombre summing up of the life of the Sheffield City Battalion: "Two years in the making. Ten minutes in the destroying. That was our history."

Remembering the store at the end of the Great War

So many people have so many memories of the store in its many guises. One lady can still recall it in 1918, just as the First World War was finally drawing to a close.

She said: "My mother always shopped at the store. I remember being taken round with her and meeting Mr Atkinson. He always used to walk around and talk to his customers. He had white whiskers and I think he wore a frock coat. As a young child I used to think he was Father Christmas!

"Lots of people in those days didn't have ready cash to spend, but used to get cheques of various values, from one pound upwards from an agent. They'd pay a fixed, weekly amount to pay it off. After that they'd start again and get another cheque.

"My mother told us Mr Atkinson lived on Prince Street, a short street which ran between Fitzwilliam Street and The Moor (long gone).

"I know I loved to be taken down the Atkinson to see Father Christmas."

Despite the war, Atkinsons continued to develop. This celebrates the opening of the new tea rooms in 1915

Last letter penned at Atkinsons

Death was ever present in the Great War.

Atkinsons worker Ada Ellen Darling wrote her last letter to her brother from the shop floor of the department store.

He died in France in October 1918, just days before the cessation of hostilities. Her hastily written note said:

"My dear 'Soldier Boy' Sidney. Excuse this paper as I am writing this at work and it is the only paper I can find. Thank you ever so much for your nice letter. You will think me a long time in answering your letter, but I did not forget you. Bless you, I am going to try and find time to make you some cakes. I get home so late at night though. I hope it is not so cold where you are as it is here."

Sadly he was dead before he got the letter. It wasn't an uncommon situation.

Atkinsons turned part of their premises over to the war effort and it was the city's women working in the factories whilst the men went to war

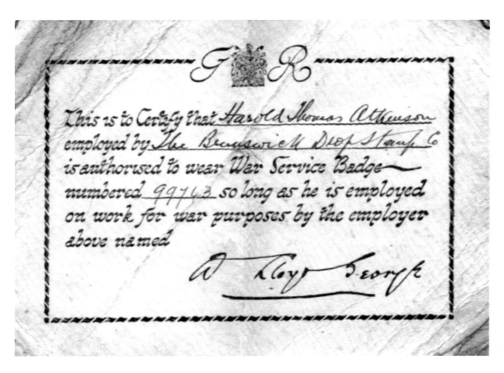

Harold Atkinson's War Service Badge authorisation signed by Lloyd George

The Sheffield Battalion that was decimated on the
first day of the Battle of the Somme

By the 1930s many of the staff were virtual personalities in their own right as their faces regularly appeared on adverts for the store and they were always on hand to greet and serve customers

CHAPTER SIX
Life in the '20s and '30s

Continued growth at Atkinsons straight after the war was very much at odds with what was happening elsewhere in the city and much of the country.

Plans for Sheffield City Hall officially ground to a halt in December 1920 before a single stone was even laid. The city simply couldn't afford it.

The economic situation was initially quite buoyant as war came to an end on November 11, 1918. Generous demobilisation bonuses were spent, returning soldiers found jobs and, for a brief moment, England seemed to be the 'fit country for heroes' promised by Prime Minister Lloyd George.

But prosperous times were short-lived.

Over-production in businesses far and wide resulted in too many goods and too few buyers. Prices slumped in 1920 and employers started to slash costs and jobs.

By the end of the year there was more than a million unemployed across the country, a third of these being ex-military.

Many soldiers were now coming straight out of the army and immediately joining the back of the dole queue. The situation was getting extremely grave. Christmas 1920 was, for many, as depressing as any in the war. The cessation of activity on the Sheffield City Hall timed with strikes, extended factory closures over the festive period and former soldiers begging on the streets, still dressed in their khaki greatcoats.

For a brief moment there were even thoughts of possible revolution - it was only three years since Russian soldiers and sailors returned from the war and seized control of the state.

Atkinsons, like they have done so many times down the years, largely bucked the trend. They continued to expand to meet unwavering demand and unveiled new and growing departments like the sprawling new Manchester (Linen) areas.

But thoughts of the Great War were never far from the minds of workers and management - former male employees had died for King and Country and many female workers were left without husbands.

The store fell silent for two minutes to mark the second anniversary of Armistice Day on November 11, 1920, like every other workplace in Sheffield.

Sheffield City Hall was originally meant as a memorial to the fallen of the city in World War One. When financial pressures forced plans to be mothballed, the cenotaph was erected in Barker's Pool. This photo shows the thousands that turned up to remember the dead on Armatice Day in the early 1920s.

Sheffield City Hall was finally unveiled in 1932 - Atkinsons have had many events in there over the years

Marking the first 50 years

By 1922 the store had a staggering 46 departments and was decked out like never before to celebrate its jubilee. A book, 'A Romance of The Moor', was published to mark the milestone.

A full time horticultural expert looked after every conceivable floral arrangement which adorned the store for the celebrations. The decorated multi-level, atrium structure, complete with glass roof, was a site to behold.

Live chickens and other livestock were housed on the ground floor, specifically to entertain the children, whilst the resident pianist and classical quartet kept the adults in good spirits.

Though the jubilee celebrations were a true boost for the store, thoughts of the war were never far away. In fact Atkinsons did its best to highlight the plight of soldiers crippled in the fighting.

Official celebrations took the form of a Luncheon and Fashion Fete on behalf of the Sheffield Cripples' Aid Association.

It was led by the Lord Mayor of Sheffield, Alderman Simpson.

A local journalist said of the event: "A great crowd packed the premises of John Atkinson's, the great Sheffield drapers on The Moor, whose jubilee celebrations were opened this afternoon by the Lord Mayor. A luncheon, at which many friends in the trade and leading citizens were present, as well as Sir David Davies, MP of Manchester, preceded the ceremony.

"For four years in succession John Atkinson's have given a special day to help the Sheffield Cripples' Aid Association, and today, as the result of a happy thought by the honoured head of the firm, Mr John Atkinson, the jubilee Celebration has been made a special day for the cripples."

An estimated 8 million people were left disabled after WW1. Scores of charities were set up to help their plight but many struggled to give them what they really wanted, employment and self-respect.

Atkinsons set aside their whole jubilee day to help. The only business being done that day was by the casualties of the war. Around 40 of them were at work in the store making mats, baskets and flower arranging.

John Atkinson was now in his mid-seventies but was showing no sign of slowing down.

The store was truly breathtaking. As you walked past the entrance fountain you'd soon realise Atkinsons offered virtually everything you'd ever wish for to make your home life complete.

Departments included medicines and perfumes, domestic ironmongery, baby linen, robe and gown, boys' tailoring and outfitting and, as popular today as it ever was, its in-house restaurant.

Though Atkinsons was a happy ship internally, life wasn't such a bed of roses elsewhere in the country. The 1926 General Strike was just around the corner and by 1930 unemployment in the country had increased from one million to two and a half million.

Sheffield was worse hit than most. Its steel and heavy industries were reliant on the export market. Order books became empty almost overnight. Jobs at Atkinsons were a godsend for many.

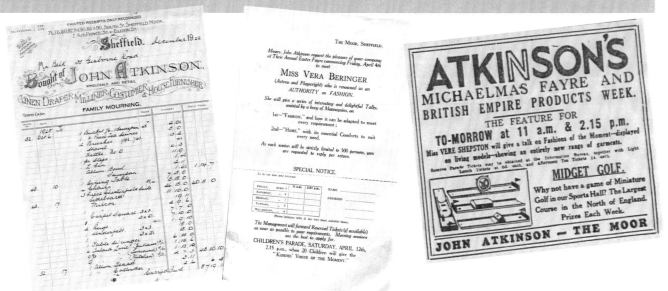

An "irreplaceable loss" and the end of an era

John Atkinson, at the age of 84, died on March 14, 1929. Though it was a time of great political and economic turmoil on the national and world stage, his amazing store was still going from strength to strength. Many called him an "irreplaceable loss" but,

before long, his successors would soon prove the entrepreneurial spirit was alive and well in a whole long line of Atkinsons.

His memorial service was held at Carver Street Chapel, just a few minutes walk from the store.

John Atkinson on holiday in his later years

THREE MEN OF THE MOOR.

John Atkinson pictured alongside his two sons who were now a key part of the business

Memories of John Atkinson

Mrs Lillian G. Hill said: "I worked in the store in 1921 and can well remember the founder, a very old gentleman who still lived on the premises, looked after by a housekeeper and houseman.

"Sir, as we called him, used to shuffle round the department on the busiest days amongst the customers and popped out the lift at all times. We'd rush to help him whenever we saw him.

"I remember on one occasion being employed on a new cosmetic enterprise, and going to his aid with a small container in my hand holding lemon night cream.

"He asked me how much it cost. When I told him it was 2s 6d he snorted and said: 'Do they ask you if it is made of gold?'"

John Atkinson was known to be quite blunt with customers in his later years. He said to one lady who couldn't find a hat to suit her that it "must be her face, not his stock" that was the reason!

Entertaining Sheffield

The 1930s saw a true entertainment revolution on the streets of Sheffield.

Talking films appeared for the first time at scores of cinema houses right across the city and it was the start of a true boom time for the silver screen.

The city centre has had some varied sights over the years but few top the marauding tiger that was at large on December 2, 1933. It was out of its cage for a full four hours after it decided a trip round town was far more preferable to being locked up at the Empire Theatre, sited just up The Moor from Atkinsons.

In 1935, SWFC not only reached the FA Cup Final, they actually won it.

SUFC were in the final the following year – unfortunately they lost.

Other spectator sports were also hugely popular. The city had a baseball team (Sheffield Dons); a national boxing champion (Johnny Cuthbert); 10,000 turned to witness the first greyhound meeting at Owlerton Stadium and Bramall Lane still doubled as a cricket ground.

If we weren't watching it we were taking part. The open air pool at Millhouses Park was a very popular pastime; though men and women were not allowed to swim together. Many problematic issues of today were already making negative headlines back then.

The car was already a serious problem. In 1930 alone, seventy people were killed in road accidents in the city with a further 1,500 injured.

Traffic congestion was already a major issue and Belisha beacon pedestrian crossings made their Sheffield debut in 1934, together with 30 miles an hour speed limits.

Film stars Laurel and Hardy visited the city in 1932 and made personal appearances at the Cinema House.

Starting at Atkinsons in 1936

Megan Smith (nee Scott) remembers the store of the 1930s being "lovely and tiered". She started there in 1936.

She said: "I served a kind of apprenticeship and worked in all the offices. I started on three shillings a week and ended up spending most of my working life working there.

"We were always provided with morning coffee, a lovely lunch and tea break. If it was late night Friday or Saturday we'd also get a high tea.

"The Atkinsons were very nice people. I remember the mantle department with its coats and suits. There was the gown department with its beautiful carpets. All departments had a display in the middle of them."

Another war made Sheffield prosperous

The one thing the country most feared, another war, was actually the city's saviour in terms of its economy.

By the mid-1930s the Sheffield steel mills were once again in full production in a bid to catch up with Hitler who was re-arming his country at an alarming rate. The Treaty of Versailles, agreed after World War One to ensure Germany was stripped of the ability to wage war again, was effectively in tatters.

Though the dark shadow of war was looming once again, business was flourishing in Atkinsons.

There were festivities galore in 1935 to celebrate the Silver Jubilee of His Majesty, King George V. A commemorative booklet given away by Atkinsons said he'd reigned over "the most eventful twenty-five years in the world's history". Sadly, the rise of the Nazis would soon be overshadowing that.

It was around this time that the founder's grandsons, R. G. Atkinson and J. H. Atkinson joined the company.

The opening of a new children's gallery at Atkinsons, in front of 700 people, was another sign of prosperous times in the 1930s in Sheffield.

The store offered prizes to the babies born nearest to the opening day. Mrs Brocklehurst of Pitsmoor won a deluxe perambulator (a pram to you or I) as her baby was born within an hour of the opening!

Photos taken
for the store's
50th anniversary
celebrations in 1922

Photos taken
for the store's
50th anniversary
celebrations in 1922

John Atkinson's Millinery Show Room, 76 to 90, The Moor.

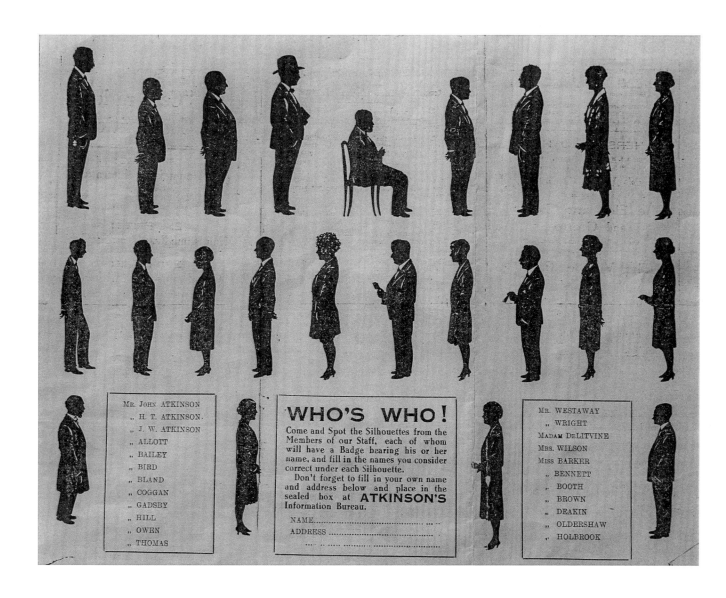

WHO'S WHO!

Come and Spot the Silhouettes from the Members of our Staff, each of whom will have a Badge bearing his or her name, and fill in the names you consider correct under each Silhouette.

Don't forget to fill in your own name and address below and place in the sealed box at **ATKINSON'S** Information Bureau.

NAME.. ... ..

ADDRESS .... -

....

MR. JOHN ATKINSON
 „ H. T. ATKINSON.
 „ J. W. ATKINSON
 „ ALLOTT
 „ BAILEY
 „ BIRD
 „ BLAND
 „ COGGAN
 „ GADSBY
 „ HILL
 „ OWEN
 „ THOMAS

MR. WESTAWAY
 „ WRIGHT
MADAM DeLITVINE
MRS. WILSON
MISS BARKER
 „ BENNETT
 „ BOOTH
 „ BROWN
 „ DEAKIN
 „ OLDERSHAW
 „ HOLBROOK

Baron Scotford, the eminent silhouettist designed this silhouette quiz from 1920. Prizes ranged from a bedroom suite of furniture, a real mole fur coat, a handsome Gilbert cabinet gramophone, free silk stockings for a year and 100 consolation prizes.

Celebration Week was a sale to behold

The shape of retail has changed beyond all recognition over recent years and sales - in many shops at least - seem to be almost year long.

Atkinsons have always tried to keep their events a bit special and their sales of today are the highlight of the calendar for many.

In the earlier part of the last century celebrations around sales would regularly attract the interest of local journalists.

The Yorkshire Telegraph & Star reported of one: "There is a crowded, bustling atmosphere about the departments of Messrs. John Atkinson on The Moor, which at once causes people to realise there is much ado about something. The store is "gailey" dressed as for a festival, and on every side there are alluring displays of wearing-apparel or household furnishings labelled with cards marked "Celebration Week"- "Special Bargain Offer" or "Free Gift No: So-and-So". When anyone made a purchase they were given a numbered gift card and it was their job to try and match the number with one of over 300 items on display - if it matched it was their item to keep.

And these weren't bargain basement gifts either. A "fumed oak bedroom suite" was the most valuable - at that point still unclaimed - and one lady had just won a "coney seal coat" which had been on proud display in the shop window.

Prams, bedsteads, gramophones... The list went on! Graham Frith, manager of Atkinsons, says inventive sales periods and unique promotions have been a cornerstone of the store's success down the decades. "Our "Blue Pencil" was first devised in the 1960s and lasted just one day in January and another in July. On these particular days the store was so full that staff needing to get from the rear of the store to the front (or vice versa) had to travel round the outside of the building. It wasn't unknown for customers to argue, or even fight, over who had the right to purchase a particular "one off". "

Atkinsons sponsor the Weekly Telegraph's Cookery Book

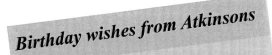

Mrs. S. South remembers: "When I was a girl, if you gave your name and address and birthday to Atkinsons they sent a birthday card from 'Uncle John'.
"My mother did this for me and I still have the card sent in 1930."

A birthday card sent by John Atkinson

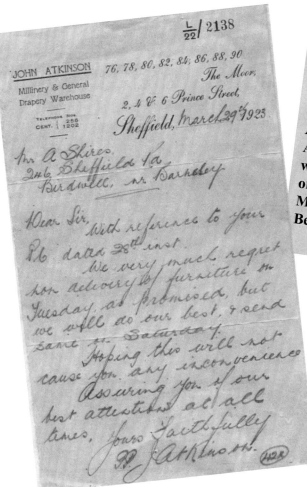

The volume of deliveries in the mid-1920s shows just how successful the operation was. A fleet of John Atkinson vans was dropping off goods to every corner of Sheffield on a daily basis. From Totley to Attercliffe, everywhere was covered.

And they didn't stop there. Kiveton Park to Worksop were covered on Fridays; Clowne and Chesterfield on Wednesdays and Hathersage and Castleton on a Monday.

Best of all, most deliveries were free

Atkinsons were renowned for their efficient deliveries. It wasn't unusual for John Atkinson to write personally in the event of a delay!

A whistle-stop tour of Atkinsons

In the New Year of 1926 Atkinsons were giving away a "pictorial tour" of the shop to encourage "closer acquaintance with our store". It came in the shape of a calendar and blotter.

The keepsake gives an amazing insight into the look and feel of the first, purpose-built Atkinsons shop.

It said: "The whole of our store is planned in a systematic manner so as to make shopping easy and convenient. On the ground floor, for example, you will find every variety of fabric for personal wear and for the home.

"The handsome glass showcases not only give brilliance and colour to the store, but greatly assist customers in making their choice and in suggestions for future occasions.

"Luxury" and "comfort" were the bywords for Atkinsons shoppers. Here was their advice on buying a coat:

"It is a serious business that requires willing assistants, sufficient privacy and plenty of moving room so that the garment may be viewed through mirrors from every angle. Thick, soft carpets and restful loungers give luxury and comfort to our mantle department."

Knitwear was booming in the period. Atkinsons said: "Children always look their prettiest in knitted garments. The little Brechette Suits with coat and cap to match are perfectly fascinating. Jumper suits with novel trimmings and colour combinations are cosy for mother, too."

It was as equally popular for the ladies. The publicity material said: "The firm hold that knitted wear has taken on the affections of women of all grades of society has been one of the most remarkable developments of recent years. It has undoubtedly come to stay, for these garments, besides being comfortable to wear, are now manufactured to meet every passing mood of fashion in colours and styles. From somewhat clumsy garments, they have become the last word in smart and becoming effect."

An Englishman's home might have been his castle but, as far as Atkinsons were concerned, a woman's dressing table took centre stage in the 1930s home in Sheffield. The publicity material continued: "Dressing table equipment of today is a thing of beauty. The powders, creams and perfumes on which the modern woman sets such store are irresistibly attractive in their dainty packings.

"We find that our Drug Department, with its great variety of necessities for external and internal use, is much appreciated by ladies. They value the opportunity of being able to satisfy their varied requirements under one roof!"

There's no doubt the "gown salon" and "fur department" were two of the most luxurious areas. As publicity material said: "Now we will take you to the first floor where you will find garments of all kinds ready to wear. It is a very attractive floor with the open gallery running round the big well under the dome.

"In our fur department we have a particular pride, for by skilled buying and expert knowledge we have established a high reputation far and wide. At our periodical fur sales we offer bargains that are really remarkable. We have our own staff of skilled furriers who can make up furs to meet all requirements and present them with the beautiful finish always associated with high-class work."

Even underclothing had come of age. "From being ugly garments of torture, and the cause of much ill-health, the corset in these days is a beautiful production that gracefully conforms to the natural lines of the figure, and gives freedom of movement, suppleness, and ease. In a modern corset suited to her figure, a woman has a wonderful sense of well being and a feeling of support, which, while not pressing on any vital organs or causing her to become misshapen, gives her that graceful and erect carriage which is so admired today." Though women felt very at home in a department store like Atkinsons, the men, it seemed, were rather more coy in their shopping habits. Atkinsons were happy to oblige.

"Men are shy creatures in a general store. Give them a secluded department for their own requirements, attended by sympathetic salesmen, and they are happy."

The Atkinsons tour concluded that there was little they didn't supply that you were ever going to need in life...

"... They will clothe you, your wife, sons and daughters, and set them up in everything the heart desires, equal to the shops of London and Paris at prices that bear comparison anywhere.

"...They will furnish your house, from cellar to attic, be it cottage or mansion in the perfect taste.

"...They will provide a delightful hour for you and your friends in their restaurant.

"...They will supply you with Ironmongery and China to range from Scullery to Dining Room.

"...They can bring "tears of joy" with their toys to your own and to your friends' children.

"... Their service in the New Hairdressing Department is already a recognised fact. Your enquiries are dealt with by fully qualified assistants."

Official 1922 Golden Jubilee Photograph, with John Atkinson front, centre, leaning on his umbrella

Saturday shopping in Sheffield

There's no doubt allegiance to SUFC or SWFC dictated the shape of Saturday afternoons for a large percentage of families in the pre-war years.

But, if the season was finished, a trip into town shopping was the favoured option for many with Atkinsons normally high on the agenda.

This is how Mrs. Sheila Rodman remembers it:

"If there wasn't a match on, Dad and Alan would go shopping with us and sometimes we would go down to the Open Market at the bottom of Dixon Lane, where I loved looking at the animals and birds in cages. I wouldn't now though. Poor little things. It never occurred to anyone then how cruel it was, I suppose.

"We would then go to the pictures either at the Hippodrome on Cambridge Street or the Central Picture House on the Moor.

"We would finally end up in Atkinsons on the top floor where there was a mock-Tudor cafe [named The Tudor Rooms]. This was a great place to be because there was a central space in the shop right down to the lower ground floor and each of the four floors had balconies running right round so that you could sit at your tea table and look at all the shoppers below as they wandered around. I always had a drink of milk and soda. A strange combination, but for some reason I loved it and would sit there happily eating my sandwiches and sipping my drink as I watched the activity all around me.

"I loved Atkinsons particularly because at Easter they had an area at the end of the ground floor which was covered with artificial grass and had a miniature switchback to ride on. There were also little live yellow chicks and baby bunnies scampering about. Of course there were always Easter eggs of all shapes and sizes too. The other lovely thing for a small child was Father Christmas in his special grotto, when you could sit on his knee and tell him what kind of present you would like. I was never able to forgive our Church School headmaster for telling us there was no such thing as Father Christmas. Marks and Spencer was just above Atkinsons off The Moor, across a small alley, and Mum used to buy my Whitsuntide best frocks from there.

"After all this lovely day we would catch the tramcar home. Tired but happy. It was a great way to spend Saturdays and will always be a vivid memory for me."

1922 advert

The stylish splendour of Atkinsons is displayed to its full potential in this 1926 complimentary blotter and calendar

CHAPTER SEVEN
Blitzed beyond recognition

Total devastation - decades of work wiped out in one single night

The night of Thursday, December 12/13, 1940, changed the face of Sheffield city centre for ever. It was the population's worst nightmare confirmed.

We were already more than a year into war with Germany, France had fallen and Britain was bracing itself for the very real threat of invasion by Germany.

By late autumn of that year the only saving grace was the worsening weather which was making it more and more likely that an invasion by Hitler's armies would be delayed until the spring of 1941.

Sheffield had always assumed it was high on Germany's hit list, the strength of its armaments factories made it an obvious target.

But despite the bombing of the likes of Coventry, Liverpool, Birmingham and London; Steel City remained generally unscathed.

Everything changed on the evening of December 12/13. Earlier that day, Sheffielders had made up their minds to put thoughts of conflict to the back of their minds that night and start celebrating Christmas in earnest.

Thursday was half-day closing and by teatime there were thousands of people pouring back into the city centre on their way to cinemas, dances at the City Hall and Cutlers Hall, the pubs, hotels and other entertainment establishments.

The Moor's Central Picture House - situated on the other side of the road from Atkinsons - was showing Shirley Temple's Blue Bird that night. Parents queued in droves with their children. It was a Christmas treat. The film

was heralded as a rival to Judy Garland's Wizard of Oz.

Atkinsons was more prepared for conflict than most. They'd had a bombproof strong room installed underneath the shop to store scores of ledgers that held the accounts for the thousands of Atkinsons customers. There were no computer backups in 1940 - just irreplaceable, handwritten documentation.

The sirens first rang out across the city at 7pm. Few people batted an eyelid - there'd been that many false alarms over the last few months and people largely took the eerie drone in their stride.

When the noise of anti-aircraft fire rang out a few minutes later people began to realise this might be more serious.

In short it was the start of nine solid hours of bombing by over 300 German aircraft. There was two day's respite and then the bombers returned the following Sunday.

Over 2,000 people were killed or injured and nearly a tenth of the city's population were made homeless over the two nights of hell. There was hardly a suburb of the city that wasn't hit.

Bombsites remained for years. The telltale signs still remain, nearly 75 years on.

Atkinsons, like the rest of the shops in Sheffield city centre that cold winter's day on December 12, 1940, was decked out with glittering Christmas window displays as the hours to blackout closed in.

Dorothy Welsby said: "Atkinsons was always renowned for its glittering window displays and the build up to Christmas, 1940, was no different. I remember an amazing array of fur coats, toys and festive decorations. It was the kind of nice thing that helped you forget there was a war on. We were always grateful for small pieces

Joyce Spurr said: "When I saw The Moor, I was appalled as it was a blazing inferno with the black skeletons of trams silhouetted against the flames. There were lumps of debris and cables hanging down. It made such a vivid impression on me that the image remained with me for the rest of my life."

Devastation of the Sheffield Blitz

Nearly 75 years on and it's hard to imagine the sheer devastation endured by the people of Sheffield on those two fateful nights.

On the roads there were 31 trams and 22 buses destroyed or severely damaged. Tramwires were broken in 30 places and 857 street lamps were either destroyed or damaged.

Eight schools were razed to the ground with a further ten badly damaged; 18 churches were destroyed with many other damaged

Priority was given to feeding and finding accommodation for people who had lost their homes, clearing roads, getting public transport restarted and knocking down dangerous buildings in the days that followed.

Surrey Street's Central Library was set up an information bureau to help residents with their post-Blitz problems.

Bombed-out shops and businesses made hasty arrangements to start up in alternative premises.

Defiance was in the air – everybody threw themselves behind the business of clearing up.

Scores of stories of bravery by rescue squads, nurses, fire fighters, ambulance drivers, police, air raid wardens and members of the public started to emerge.

Sheffield's behaviour in the Blitz was held up as an example to all in a 1942 Ministry of Information booklet.

Walsh's store - another victim of the Blitz

of normality like that."

By the early hours of December 13, 1940, Hitler had totally destroyed everything Atkinsons had worked for over the past 68 years. Raid after raid had turned the store into a pile of smouldering rubble and twisted metal. The only recognisable aspect of the store was the two pinnacles that still stood in defiance against the Nazi attack.

Despite all this, management were still confident that their impenetrable, underground vault had kept their irreplaceable customer records safe.

George Hennings was a firewatcher at nearby Robert Brothers store - few people had a better view of Atkinsons that night. This is his harrowing eye witness account:

"From the roof I could see many fires. Near this very spot, at the top of Matilda Street, ¬Wilson's the wholesale tobacconists shop was well alight. Looking up Pinstone Street I could see Campbell's furniture store was a blazing mass, flames leaping many feet high. At this time there seemed to be plenty of water available. About this hour I took a group of firemen for some hot milk as they were nearly frozen. It was bitterly cold.

"Then we were informed that water was scarce and shortly afterwards it went off altogether for the night. What a tragedy! Sticking to my duty, I went back to the shop and for a brief period nothing exciting happened. Going on to the roof again, I could see all around -

Heeley, Millhouses, Abbeydale - what a position. Here I was, helpless as a child, unable to do anything to avert disaster, which I felt sure would befall the very place I was in. Down below my men were wandering about demented with fear. I realised they could only be a hindrance to me and by no means a help, so I bade them go home.

"Nine o'clock! The danger grew nearer and nearer and yet our store remained whole; so far as I could perceive there was no damage - not so much as a window cracked. Going to the front of the shop, about 9.30pm, I looked down The Moor and saw to my horror many shops and trams ablaze. Then I realised what a Blitz meant to us in Sheffield. At this time there was very little wind stirring and the fires were confined to the bottom end of The Moor. I could hear bombs falling in the distance and see fires starting in many more districts. Back I went to the roof of our own store and remained there until midnight.

"Then I realised that I could feel in no way safe at such a

height, with the possibility of every avenue of escape cut off. Just at this time I was hit by a piece of shrapnel. It must have been from a shell bursting in the air near our building. A coping stone bore marked evidence of this, for about two feet of stone was chipped out. Fortunately for me I wore my steel helmet. To say I was grateful is altogether too mild an expression.

"At about 12.30am, a great change took place - bombs fell everywhere, or so it seemed. Everyone was in a state of excitement and, by this time, flames were steadily creeping up The Moor. A strong wind rose at this hour and fanned the blaze into something like fury. Debris was falling all around and our store got its first shock. A great tremor caused by a bomb exploding nearby blasted out our great windows. Glass and woodwork was flying around us like hail in a whirling storm. Happily, I escaped with just a few minor injuries, which a drop of iodine relieved for the moment

At this period we became isolated from every power: gas, electricity and water. The wind came up The Moor with a great force - like a hurricane, helping the flames along; yet it was bitterly cold. All the buildings were ablaze - Atkinsons, Darley's, Gebhart's, Langton's and many others. I, along with others, could only watch and wait in fear and trembling, wondering as to what would be our fate.

"From this time onwards bombs of every type seemed to fall continuously. Standing outside, opposite our store, I saw many things happen around me which made me feel anything but brave, and yet, like a lad in the last war, I was "afraid to be afraid". It was all so frightful, so fiendishly indescribable.

"Firemen, Ambulance men, A.R.P. Wardens, and workers and all branches of the Civil Defence were

The Moor in the aftermath of the Blitz

doing their bit and doing it well. Many people were trapped in shelters under shops. Sulphur and burning materials made these untenable, and still everyone stuck to the job in hand, whilst destruction played its fiendish part.

"At about 2am a very old man came across to me. He told me he was the watchman at Woolworths and whilst he was sitting in the cellar, a bomb about the size of a

fire extinguisher came through the shop floor into the cellar. He coolly said, "I knelt down to examine it and heard something ticking inside so thought I better come out of the premises". Woolworth's blew up at 2.30 am. The bomb was a time bomb! If I had not advised the man to stay out, he would have gone back.

The King and Queen arrive in Sheffield to assess the damage

"At this time, a fire brigade officer and I went to the Central Picture Palace and got in touch with the water department by telephone, but we were given to understand the position was hopeless as to water supply, and: still the work of destruction, both by fire and bombs, went on. At this time, the Germans were machine-gunning the Moorhead area.

"The Moor up to Rockingham Street was well alight. Atkinsons was burning furiously. I stood at the top of Matilda Street and wondered what would be the outcome. Near to me, a fireman had been blown across the road. When found he was badly wounded; his leg had been blown off. For six months he was in hospital. He is now employed in the Fire Office as a telephone operator. He has been fitted with an aluminium leg.

"News of the disaster passed on from one part of the city to the other from time to time, and still there was no chance of water to extinguish the fires raging in the surrounding buildings. It was now dangerous to be in the open for debris and shrapnel was flying in all directions. The Moor was one huge mass of flames. Right and left, in most parts gas mains and electricity mains were torn up.

"Above our store, at 3.45am, Bray's and Binns, and the rest of the shops in Button Lane were well alight, starting one after the other. Redgates, part of Berry's Vaults, Woolworths, The Devonshire, and other places were going one after the other in explosion and fire. Rats and cats were fleeing in all directions, but never once did I see a dog the whole night through. Then our fate grew gradually nearer. Material in flames was flying up The Moor, helped by a wind like a hurricane. This blew through every window - and still we were unscathed.

"Just before 4am a sergeant fireman and I were standing by Burton's the Tailors looking up to our roof opposite. We saw small fires starting in the mantle and dressmaking workshop. "We rushed across and for a time fought the flames with all the means at our disposal including extinguishers, sand and any water available. We succeeded in getting the fire out for a while. Soon after 4am we turned downstairs to see what else we could do. Looking through the mantle department we saw at the extreme end of the store, the millinery department, and all that end was enveloped in flames. We could do no more, for the heat was intense and the smoke was suffocating. We could only come out into the open, to watch from the other side.

"In ten minutes the whole building was one mass of flames. Fifty or more firemen were waiting to do their duty, but they were helpless - no water! Then about this time the "all clear" sounded. Our building went on burning. So far, no one had suffered from injury on our site.

"Many people were released from shelters in and around our district in The Moor area. Moving about the neighbourhood, one would be startled by a voice from a damaged shelter, or a cellar grate, asking if the "all clear" had sounded. And oh, what strange sights greeted us everywhere. Men and women blackened with soot and smoke and powder blast. Destruction, devastation, everywhere. And, by God's grace, here we were spared!"

Faithful friend was final purchase

When Cyril Dodgson arrived at Atkinsons just seconds before half-day closing on the lunchtime of Thursday, December 12, he'd no idea his purchase would go down in the store's history.

He worked at Richard. W. Carr. & Co Ltd. at Wadsley Bridge and was on his way home to Nether Green but decided to stop off at the store to buy a Christmas present for his daughter.

Cyril Dodgson chose a Merrythought Production Teddy Bear, just as the doors were shutting for the very last time - just hours before the bombs dropped.

His daughter, Brenda Spencer (nee Dodgson) still treasures the present to this day.

"Teddy has been a much loved, faithful friend ever since", she said

Brenda still treasures the bear to this day

Brenda cuddles the bear with her brother

A mobile canteen serves drinks to survivors in the city centre

A contemporary drawing of Atkinsons after the attacks by Sheffield artist and engraver Kenneth Steel RBA:SGA 1906-1970. Kenneth's pregnant wife, Olive, and his invalid mother were both killed in the Blitz, when the family home on Westbrook Bank took a direct hit)

Carnage looking up High Street

CHAPTER EIGHT

How Atkinsons was reborn

Atkinsons recovery in the face of total and utter devastation was a lesson for anyone who has ever had a bad day at work.

Few mornings could ever be likened to the scene that greeted staff turning up to do their jobs on Friday, 13, December 1940.

The Atkinsons were already there - they'd arrived at 5am. Though there wasn't much that could be done for the building, there was just time to release six delivery vans from the adjoining garages that were just about to go up in smoke.

The store was a pile of smouldering rubble, much of The Moor was blitzed out of existence and the area was awash with teams of fire crews that had arrived in the city from all around the region to help contain the flames and utter devastation.

Many described the popular shopping thoroughfare as looking like "a holocaust" in the aftermath of the bombing.

Though the Atkinsons store had been razed to the ground, management still believed one major investment they'd made in the run up to attacks was there to ensure cash flow could be maintained.

They'd had the foresight to install a bombproof strong room to store the ledgers that kept every scrap of information on customers and the amounts they owed the store - paying 'on tick' was very much the norm for many at that time.

Sadly, their pre-planning had not accounted for human error. In fact the morning of December 13, 1940, was the moment Atkinsons realised the luck that had been on their side since they day they opened in 1872 had finally run out.

The members of staff responsible for the strong room had forgotten to close the door on the fateful night and the majority of contents had gone up in smoke with the rest of the store.

But all, amazingly, was not lost. In fact what happened next proved just how loyal customers were to Atkinsons. It would have been easy, in light of all customer records disappearing detailing the monies that were owed on credit, for Sheffielders to not pay what they owed – something that would have probably finished the store for good.

Amazingly, totally the opposite happened.

Atkinsons store manager of today, Graham Frith, said: "Within three months of the end of the Sheffield Blitz, 80% of the money owed was paid back to us by customers, voluntarily."

The store and its staff showed amazing resilience, tenacity and spirit in the way they dealt with the situation. A meeting was convened just hours after the attacks for all managers and executives, in a garage in the Millhouses area of the city.

John Atkinson's sons, Harold and Walter Atkinson, who were now running the store, were about to show their

With no store, management set up temporary offices on Millhouses Lane

outstanding skill at improvisation.

Within a few weeks they were open for business once again in temporary premises in St Jude's Church and School room on Milton Street. They'd got a kiosk outside the railway station and their various departments were appearing everywhere from the semi-blitzed Central Cinema on The Moor to The Star and Telegraph building.

St Jude's Church and school room, at that point disused and partly derelict, became the base for further expansion

How the recovery was reported in the press at the time

THE LORD MAYOR OF SHEFFIELD (Councillor Luther F. Milner) behind the counter after opening Messrs. Atkinsons' new store in the Central Picture House, The Moor, yesterday.

into the premises of Johnson and Appleyard of Leopold Street and James Lamb on The Moor.

Credit was duly given to a small, select group of people that did their utmost to help the store get back on its feet. They included Mr Staines, manager of the Morning Telegraph, Mr. Isi Graham of the Central Cinema, City Engineer Mr Collie and Basil Gibson, the town clerk.

In 1946, a year after war ended, Atkinsons bought the high-class grocers and provision merchants Tuckwoods on Fargate. It was enlarged and turned into a department store with restaurant.

From devastation just a few years earlier, the late 1940s saw an amazing renaissance for Atkinsons. In 1947 they also bought the business of Stewart and Stewart on Pinstone Street.

In the midst of the rebuilding Mr Walter Atkinson died, in 1947, after a brief illness.

Over 500 mourners packed Millhouses Methodist Church for the funeral service.

Though the audience consisted of a large percentage of fellow retailers, the Rev. T. A. Kidd, who led the service,

was keen to emphasise another, lesser known side to Walter Atkinson; his sheer commitment to the church itself.

Both Walter and Harold's commitment to Millhouses Methodist Church lives on to this day - they both have a stained glass window installed in their name.

He said: "Those of us who only met him through business should have seen him as I have seen him - at midnight in his shirt sleeves and overalls, stoking the boiler because the caretaker was ill. It takes a great man to do that with no sense of condescension.

"There are some people we know only for a few moments and yet know through and through. He was one of those."

Fortunately, following the death of Walter, a new generation of Atkinsons - namely his grandsons, Robert, John and Edward (known as Peter) were released from their military duties and were able to join the family firm.

The store wasn't the only independent operator that recovered after the bombings.

Cockaynes, Walshs, Redgates and others also reopened in temporary premises.

Atkinsons site on The Moor remained a bombsite for the next two decades with only window facades giving an indication of what it used to be.

Megan Smith (nee Scott), who worked at Atkinsons before and after the bombings, said: "I never remembered any despondency after the Blitz. We always seemed to be at our best when there was a problem. None of us worked for a while after the Blitz. I ended up going to work in the Central Picture House on the Moor when we opened up - I ran the office there.

"The offices ended up being at Winchester House on Fargate, above Davy's. I was there when Atkinsons bought Stewart & Stewart and I used to do the accounts."

A new home for Atkinsons on High Street

Inside Tuckwoods on Fargate which was taken over by Atkinsons

A celebration on High Street

Reopenings were regularly done with fanfare to keep the spirit of Sheffield alive in spite of the devastating attacks.

As The Star reported:

"The opening, at 10 o'clock tomorrow morning of Messrs. John Atkinsons, in the centre of the city, will be an event in the history of the firm. Customers will be surprised and delighted to find the quantity of stock and the attractiveness of the new showrooms.

"The premises will be in the "Telegraph" Buildings, High Street, where they will have the use of the Sheffield Gas Company's showrooms, the directors of the Gas Company having waived their rights in order to help the city's difficulties.

"In these showrooms it will be possible to buy ladies coats and costumes, furs and fur coats, gowns and afternoon frocks, ladies shoes, millinery, gloves, hosiery, handbags, toilet requisites, and perfumery.

"The firm has also taken over premises in the Central Picture House, and hopes to open these premises shortly.

A snack bar and ladies' hairdressing department will be two of the attractions, but in addition many departments are being set up.

"It will be possible to buy at the Central, girls' and children's fashions and school outfitting, knitwear and wools, haberdashery and trimmings, furnishing and household departments, men's outfitting and silk departments.

"The Display Kiosk at the Midland Station may be transformed into an inquiry office for customers coming into the city by train and bus; and they will be told how to find the new premises."

A tram travels past the temporary windows that hid the bombsite on The Moor store for two decades

A 1948 advert

A 1951 advert

Annual Atkinsons dance at the City Hall

A 1949 advert

Christmas messages to customers in 1941 - a year after the Blitz.

Many blitzed shops had to relocate - Marks & Spencer ended up on London Road in the building later to be known as the Locarno (and these days Sainsburys)

"Undaunted" by the Blitz

Atkinsons had one of their most successful periods in the late 1940s and 1950s as they worked towards the opening of a new store and bought up other businesses. Their staff handbook of the 1960s referred to the business being "undaunted" by the attacks.

You have to admire their steely resolve. That and the way the Sheffield people rallied around a much loved retail institution.

It went on to say "temporary premises were taken in a matter of days, including the old Central Cinema which stood almost opposite and business was resumed with continued loyal service to its customers in a war scarred city.

"1941 saw the purchase of the long established furniture business of Johnson & Appleyards Ltd, whose premises in Leopold Street were quickly converted to provide a Department Store for Atkinsons. In 1946 saw the addition of Tuckwood's Stores Ltd; James Lamb & Son Ltd, of 215 The Moor, being added in 1947, followed in 1948 by the addition of Stewart and Stewart (Sheffield) Ltd."

Atkinsons also expanded their interests outside of Sheffield and bought Fletchers of Retford Ltd.

It wasn't until 1958 that it finally became possible to finalise plans for the return of Atkinsons to its original site.

Harold Atkinson with Lord Wilmot(a member of the board) celebrating the acquisition of Stewart and Stewart

Once the bomb damaged store was removed, the old site was derelict with just a facade of display windows showcasing the store for two decades

Atkinsons opens on Fargate after acquiring Tuckwoods in the aftermath of the Blitz

The former Stewart and Stewart store is reborn as Atkinsons

Fashion parades carry on regardless

Though Atkinsons were lacking a headquarters in the 1940s and 1950s, they certainly had no shortage of profile and seemed to put even greater work into their events.

The event manual for their Fashion Parade of May 21, 1957, stretched to almost 20 pages.

It left little to chance even though they were doing the whole event without any prior rehearsal. All the models were Atkinsons employees. Staff supervisor Mrs. Gibbons was running the "Welcome to Summer" event.

She, like many of the people involved, was undertaking the duties for the first time.

Mrs Gibbons summed up with thanks to: "Our bride, Sandra, from our cosmetics department; her bridesmaid, June from the Underwear Department of our Central Store; Mrs. Fisher from our Footwear Department; Mrs Searle from our Coat Department at the Central Store; Kathleen from our Montgomery Restaurant in Surrey Street and finally, our young teenager, Janet from our Office Staff."

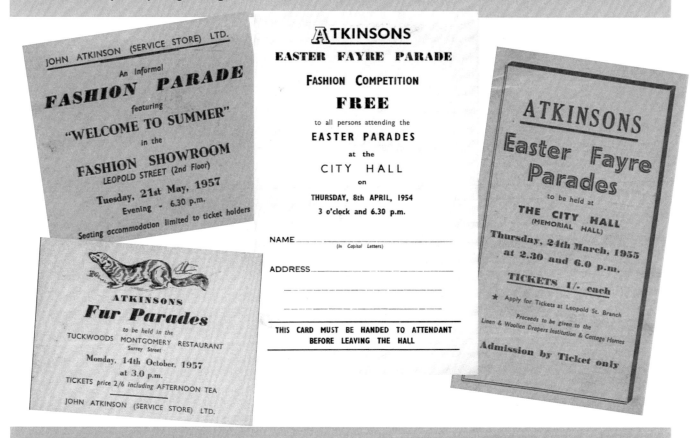

Shop girls save the day

It was scores of Atkinsons' female staff that were hard at work in the wake of the Blitz as the men folk fought overseas.

Around one third of them were immediately re-employed to fit out the likes of the room in Central Cinema, an old church and a school room that were first utilised by the store.

"The girls have been splendid", one of the managers of Atkinsons said at the time. "Willing to do anything. They have been scrubbing floors, painting, cleaning and even doing carpentry."

Gowns, mantles, millinery, shoes, gloves, hosiery and fancy goods were some of the first items to go on sale.

One employee spoke of their dismay when they saw the blitzed store: "We all felt dreadful when we came down the morning after the raid and saw the ruins of the lovely store," said the buyer in charge of the coat department, "but the firm were splendid".

Buyers were sent all over the country looking for stock. It wasn't easy, as the Atkinsons story wasn't unusual, there'd been German raids in many parts of the country and goods were in high demand.

CHAPTER NINE

The unveiling of a brand new store

The brand new store that opened in the spring of 1960. Note the tram on the extreme left of shot, the popular mode of transport reached the end of its life in Sheffield in the same year

The opening of the new Atkinsons store in the spring of 1960 marked the end of one of the final chapters in the city's recovery from the Blitz.

The vast building was unveiled to massive fanfare on the morning of Friday, February 26th.

The Star devoted an entire supplement to it the day before.

You only have to glimpse the publicity material to feel the amazing confidence and vibrancy running through the company at that point as they finally brought everything back under one roof on The Moor.

The newspaper referred to it as "a new era in city shopping". It went on to describe every aspect of the store:

"A colonnade of white and black terrazzo pillars stretching for over 100ft, forms the frontage of the store, which extends in depth from The Moor to Button Lane - more than 300ft.

"The store, which stands on the site of the old Atkinsons store destroyed 20 years ago in the Blitz, is a tall, white building, erected by one of the most up to date methods - believed to have been used in Sheffield for the first time.

"It will house, under one roof, all the Atkinsons stores at present scattered in and around the centre of the city, although the present warehouse and garages in Milton Street will remain."

The store itself was opened by Mrs. Walter Atkinson, the oldest member of the family at that point, assisted by Mr A Wright, who was the glass and china buyer who'd been with the store 54 years. They did the honours at 9.30am precisely.

The most famous person in attendance that day was celebrated actress/Eurovision song contest presenter Katie Boyle.

She spent a long time perusing the store and picking

The opening of the new store by Mrs Walter Atkinson, with sons Peter (left) and John in attendance - 20 years after the store was bombed out of existence

"lovely things" for her journey home - made even lovelier by the fact she assumed her celebrity status would bypass the need for paying!

19-year-old David Grix was head chef at the new self service eatery.

Though tender in years he'd no shortage of experience. He was former assistant chef at the Montgomery restaurant, another strand of the Atkinsons business at that time.

Two course meals were offered in the new restaurant at just two shillings. Atkinsons were even offering 'brunch' - described as a "combination of breakfast and lunch which consists of bacon, eggs and sausages".

Restaurant decor consisted of "a deep pile carpet of pale cinnamon and matching floral curtains".

Other touches included Formica topped tables "in gay colours contrasting the black ceiling over the service counter".

It was named the Fitzwilliam Restaurant and was also available for dinner dances in the evening and came complete with bar (not open in the day).

In short, the store couldn't have been more cutting edge and thought provoking. It was the first self-service store in the city and only the second one with an escalator - the first being Banners in Attercliffe. It was returning to its position as a destination in itself, a true cornerstone of Sheffield's retail experience.

There's no doubt 1960 was a pivotal year for the city. Whilst it signalled a new era for Atkinsons, it also signalled the end of the tram system in Sheffield.

Atkinsons store reflected an end to post-war austerity: high fashion, furs, upmarket homeware and more was on offer and in demand.

There was also a resident Max Factor beauty consultant; new greeting card section with its own in-house post box and stamp machine and a "self service carpet unit". Children that had grown up playing in the bombsites were starting to make their mark in the era. Peter Stringfellow was cutting his teeth as a pop promoter; Jimmy Crawford was the city's first chart star closely followed by Dave Berry and future star Joe Cocker was gigging as Vance Arnold.

It was an exciting time to be growing up and Atkinsons was a key stop off point for the young as well as the old. The Beatles were playing groundbreaking gigs in the city and glitzy cabaret clubs like Bank Street's Cavendish would help make life for the average Sheffielder more aspirational than ever thought possible just a few years earlier.

And for every taste, Atkinsons was there.

Dave Manvell said: "The opening of the new Atkinsons store was a massive event at the time. Everyone was talking about it. So many children had grown up knowing nothing but a bombsite where the original purpose-built store was. To see it finally rebuilt and reopen caused massive celebration."

Though Sheffield was embracing the enlightened sixties, it still relied on its heavy industrial base throughout the era and the city still became a virtual ghost town on the traditional two week annual shutdown as everyone boarded a Sheffield United Tour bus for the coast.

There might have been peacetime on the streets of the city throughout the era but there was one natural disaster to contend with, the Sheffield Hurricane of February 16, 1962. Though there was widespread damage across the city and fatalities, Atkinsons escaped largely unscathed.

Patricia Eales said: "I must admit the austerity years never really stopped in our house in Fir Vale, they carried on well into the sixties! But it didn't stop us window shopping. The fashions in the new look store were absolutely breathtaking. I can still remember them to this day."

Harold misses the unveiling but undoubtedly made his mark

Sadly, a key part of the Atkinsons story was not there to see the new building unveiled.

Harold Atkinson, regularly described as "the man that made The Moor", died just a few months before the new store was unveiled. He passed away at his Milllhouses Lane home on December 12, 1958. He was 79.

He learnt the retail trade from the ground up. Harold Atkinson could be found sweeping the floors of the store at 16. He joined in 1904 and worked his way up to chairman of the group.

As well as heading up the company, he was a man of wide interests and won plaudits for his charity work.

Indeed, Mr. J. E. Cockayne, chairman and managing director of T.B and W. Cockayne Ltd, paid tribute at the time and said: "I think he was the most untiring worker I have known for trade charities. He was particularly interested in the Furnishing Trades Benevolent Association which he really got going, and did outstanding work.

"Mr Atkinson had a very forceful character and was active right to the end."

1962 advert

How the local press reported the retirement of the store's popular fashion buyer Miss Ann Marjorie Marshall

The store's 90th anniversary celebrations in 1962

**Atkinsons have always been renowned for their striking window displays
- here's an award being presented for one**

**Winning the hotly contested national Dairy Box competition in 1968, with Peter
Atkinson in attendance**

Picked to be "Miss Atkinson"

Christine Rockcliffe left school at 15 and got a job in the gowns department at Atkinsons, then on Leopold Street prior to the opening of the new store.

She was picked to be the first 'Miss Atkinson' when the store returned to The Moor.

" I gave bouquets of flowers to customers every hour on opening day", she said.

She has nothing but fond memories of working at the store. "It was magical. I used to get spoiled. I remember Mrs Ruth Druce - in charge of furs. She was like a mother to me. But Mrs Chapman used to frighten me to death.

"We were never allowed to sit down in the store. I remember Mrs Gibbons, staff supervisor. We'd jump to attention when Mr John [Atkinson] walked about. There was Mrs Avery and Miss Tyzack in fashion.

"Buying a fur coat was like buying a house in those days. All the family used to come down and view it!

"I remember I bought perfume with my first commission money."

'Miss Atkinson' Christine Rockcliffe fashions the store's furs in the early 1960s

The hottest ticket in town - an invite to attend the opening of the new store

Departments have come and gone over the years - the music department was a feature for many decades. It was initially in "High Court", just off the High Street

CHAPTER TEN

Muffin the Mule, Santa's Grotto and childhood memories

Advert for the store's Christmas Grotto and Toytown in the interwar years

Few memories of Atkinsons have quite the resonance as a childhood one.

The magic of the store has been lighting up the eyes of youngsters for decades - especially at Christmas. Atkinsons still boasts one of the best toy departments anywhere in Sheffield and memories of the breathtaking grotto in years gone by are still as vivid today as they were fifty years ago for many.

The pre- Second World War Christmas displays of the original purpose-built store were a dream come true for many. It was the highlight of the year for tens of thousands of children who'd travel to the store from miles around with their parents.

A train was regularly erected in store to carry Santa and offer rides.

There was also the chance to be shot out of a magic cannon. In fact nothing was too much trouble when it came to turning Atkinsons into a true winter wonderland.

Graham Frith, manager of Atkinsons, said: "Ask any Sheffielder over a certain age and they will remember the Christmas Grottos being an eagerly awaited magical experience, as was receiving an Easter Egg in a specially designed tin (which was different every year). Sitting in the top floor restaurant looking over the balcony into the central well of the pre-war store is also embedded in customer's memories along with the not too exciting yearly ritual of being fitted for school uniforms."

Easter would also herald the arrival of live animals in the basement of the original store to amuse the youngsters. One artefact that has truly stood the test of time - and one that takes many an ageing adult straight back to childhood - is Muffin the Mule.

The ride first arrived in store in the 1950s and is still in working order and used to this day!

Look out for him. He sits proudly in the bottom stairwell between the ground and first floor.

He's still only 2p a go and is one of only a handful of its kind that still exist anywhere in the world.

Muffin the Mule made his first proper TV debut just after the war in 1946. He first arrived at Atkinsons not long after and has been delighting generations of children ever since.

Virtually every Sheffielder has their own individual memory of Atkinsons down the years. Here's a few:

Steve Bush said: "Whenever I go into the shop it's like going back 50 years - in a good way. I always stick two pence in Muffin!"

Patrica Eales: "Our mother always used to take us to Atkinsons at Christmas. It was one of the biggest treats of the year. I remember it to this day."

Helen Parsons: "We always went to Santa's Grotto there at Xmas after going to Redgates toy shop to see what we wanted. I remember the multi storey car park took ages to get out of, it used to freak me and my sister out when we were small."

Paul Bower said: "I loved the Santa's Grotto ride. When I was about three or four I did sort of believe it was real!"

Donna Jackson Shillito said: "I remember hanging out in the coffee bar with my mates in the early '80s. It was cooler than the Wimpy on Fargate."

Richard Jones said: "I remember the American style coffee bar with milk shakes, pancakes and waffles. I think it was the late 1970s. Very exotic for that time."

Faye Pyke said: "I used to always meet my mum for coffee at the Massarellas coffee shop in there and my gran was obsessed with the sewing machine lady."

Deborah Muff-Rose said: "It was my Nana's favourite shop. She took me and my sister every Saturday for a milkshake and at Whitsuntide she took us there and bought us matching outfits. We joined the parade on Whit Sunday through Meersbrook Park. Lovely childhood memories."

No "love" or "dear" please

The staff handbook of the 1960s gives an insight into the true value the store has always put on its customers. There's no doubt this is a trait that has set Atkinsons apart from many rivals over the years.

Lapsing into Yorkshire slang when addressing customers was as unacceptable then as it is now.

The handbook states: "Customers must be shown every courtesy both in person and in telephone conversations. Unless a customer is well known to you, in which case he or she may be addressed by name, "Madam" or "Sir" is the correct manner of address, not "Love" or "Duck" even though this may appear acceptable for the isolated few."

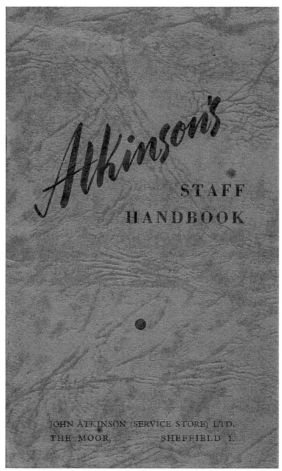

The staff handbook

And if anyone ever had any doubt as to exactly how important the customer was in the life of Atkinsons the staff handbook spelled it out:

"A customer is the most important person in our business and in our job. We do not do the customer a favour by serving her. She does us a favour by giving us the opportunity to do so - this is a fact which must never be forgotten."

Atkinsons have always been renowned as a shop that goes the extra mile for its customers. It's a passion that has been coursing through the veins of the company since its inception.

The store's archives are full of heartfelt 'thank you' letters.

One that was received May 23, 1962, for example, said: "The lady who bought a mackintosh on Monday morning wishes to thank Messrs John Atkinsons for the lovely spray of flowers which were presented to her by the charming 'Miss Atkinson'. I'd also like to thank the pleasant lady assistant for her help in choosing a mac."

Until recently it was traditional that members of the Atkinsons family were addressed as 'Mister' then their first name.

Prior to the Second World War the family would have worn frock coats whilst in store.

Tom Thumb Zoo

Atkinsons have always done their utmost to keep the children amused but it's unlikely there'll be a repeat of the attraction that ended up with a baby crocodile loose in the store!

The Tom Thumb Zoo resided in the basement of the store in the 1930s.

Sidney Wright, an electrician's assistant in the store, recalled the attraction he helped build years later.

He said: "It was an Easter attraction and it consisted of about 12 or 15 white eggs, each about 20 inches in diameter and 24 inches long, mounted on displays with all sorts of small animals inside them.

"One had rabbits inside it, there were a dozen grass snakes in another, two adders in a third, and one had a baby crocodile in it.

"There was some merriment when the grass snakes escaped. The girls in the store were scared and, as electrician's lad, I had to catch them. When the zoo finished the baby crocodile was lost. We found it dead in the lift shaft."

A job for life as part of the Atkinsons family

Few retail businesses in the region have the ability to retain staff like Atkinsons. Store manager, Graham Frith, is now one of their longest serving employees.

He explains: "We regularly receive enquires about particular individuals when families are researching their ancestry and in some instances are able to help if the person in question has worked for Atkinsons over a long period of time. A lot of information and records were destroyed in the Blitz, unfortunately, which limits the knowledge of the early years of the business.

"Many workers began their careers here in a lowly capacity, rising through the ranks to achieve prominence. Here are just a few from the modern era...

"Margaret Peacock joined during the centenary year of 1972 as a filing clerk. Her tasks as office manager are made simpler by today's modern technology.

"Sally Stanley, the human resources manager, began as a Christmas temp in 1988 on the seasonal goods section.

"Brian King started work in the records and electrical shop on High Court (just off High Street) and retired in 2012 as company secretary and director after 54 years of service.

"Margaret Ryan worked here for 45 years, retiring in 1984.

"Sandra Shaw, the present household linens and seasonal gifts buyer, has been with Atkinsons for 35 years and remembers her early days on the DIY department where she happily cut wood to size on a circular saw if her male colleagues were unavailable. In the Cookshop she remembers a customer returning a non-stick fry pan with a fried egg still attached and pressure cooker complete with stew inside because the lid couldn't be removed. Her introduction to her newly promoted position as linens "under buyer" was marked by a customer puncturing a pressure packed bean bag of polystyrene pellets with a stiletto heel resulting in an explosion of them statically stuck to her. "Looking like a snowman, the situation was made worse by attempts to brush them off. Luckily she, staff and customers alike saw the funny side and were convulsed with laughter until a handy Hoover provided the solution.

"Not only have many staff been attached to Atkinsons for several decades, you can often hear customers remark that they were first brought to the store as children by their parents and continue to visit with their offspring.

"Much of the social activities of the store were, until the 1970s, run by Mrs Eliza Flynn who ruled the warehouses and transport sections with a no nonsense approach that won the respect of all the men under her control.

"Early social activities would have included visits by bus on half day closing to local Derbyshire beauty spots or market towns.

"Dinner dances from 1960 were actually held in the store's restaurant which provided for functions out of store hours. If you ever find you have a "spring in your step" walking to the present first floor restaurant it's because the dance floor is still under part of the furniture department.

"Other social activities were many and various from summer 'salmon and strawberry' evenings at Baldwins Omega restaurant, medieval banquets perfected by Eckington Hall or involvement in charity nights, runs, snooker marathons and a particularly wet raft race on what was the new Rother Valley Country Park (a far healthier one compared to the ones previously held on Sheffield canal, pre Victoria Quays and the big clean up)."

Famous faces at Atkinsons

There has been no shortage of VIPs shopping at Atkinsons down the decades.

It was a hit with two of the city's most recognisable chart-toppers - Martin Fry of ABC and Phil Oakey of the Human League.

Snooker star John Virgo, football star Tony Currie, boxing hero Herol 'Bomber' Graham and X Factor winner Shayne Ward have all frequented the store.

It has been the setting for book launches, TV programmes, celebrity chef displays and more besides.

Graham Frith, store manager, said: "Management have always strived to create a "family" atmosphere amongst staff (whether front of house or behind the scenes) which filters through to the store.

"As most customers have been loyal, regular patrons throughout their adult life, they feel part of the "family". Staff are encouraged to foster friendships with regular customers, be on first name terms and make them feel welcome and relaxed. "

Muffin the Mule, remembered and ridden on by many generations

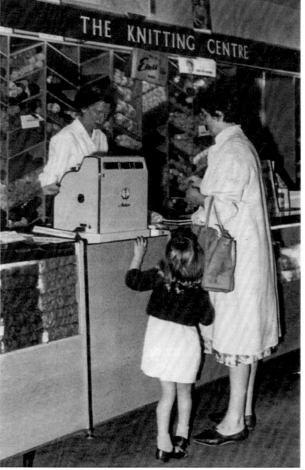

The store's popular Knitting Centre with Margaret Ryan, a sales assistant for 45 years

CHAPTER ELEVEN
The booming '70s

Sheffield's retail sector has had its up and downs over the decades but few would argue that the seventies were one of its more successful.

Atkinsons in the 1970s - a flagship retailer throughout the decade

True to form, Atkinsons was a retail flagship of the era. In fact it makes you wonder if John Atkinson was weaving his magic from beyond the grave - there couldn't have been a more buoyant year for the store's centenary celebrations than 1972!

It's fair to say the mere thought of Meadowhall in the era would have been laughed off the high street.

It wouldn't have stood a chance.

Sheffield city centre offered a shopping experience like nowhere else in the land. It was a true destination.

People would travel from right around the region – often right across the country – to sample it.

It offered every conceivable type of shop and, as well as Atkinsons, boasted other major independent household name department stores with histories stretching back decades: Cockaynes, Redgates and Walsh's for example.

Sheffield Town Hall's publicity department rightly crowned the city as 'the shopping centre of the north'.

There was a city-centre-wide annual competition to find the Lady Sales Assistant of the Year and the Saleswomen of the Year organised by the city's Junior Chamber of Trade in those pre-politically correct times.

The confidence in Sheffield at that point was incredible – it was truly lining up to sell itself to the world. The Town Hall were determined to change "the world-wide image of Sheffield as a row of back-to-back terraced houses and cobbled streets punctuated by the smokiest steel works in Europe".

The size and audacity of the city's marketing drive seems hard to believe forty years or so on.

In 1971 a Sheffield exhibition, City On The Move, was unveiled at London's Royal Exchange.

Opened by the then Lord Mayor of London, Sir Peter Studd, it was designed to bring the capital's public up to date with Sheffield. Retail was a key part of it.

And far from living in the shadow of nearby cities like Leeds, Manchester and Nottingham, Sheffield took the retail fight to them.

The council blitzed Leeds with festive carrier bags in a bid to bag Christmas trade with the message – "Shop in Sheffield this Christmas!" - much to the shock of their rivals!

Over 350,000 stickers were produced as part of the campaign to bring tourists, conference organisers, shoppers and industrialists into the city to see what it had to offer.

The first batch of ten different designs used headings such as "Emerging City", "City Of Skills And Quality", "The Clean Air City" and of course, "The Shopping Centre of the North".

It was one of the most successful PR campaigns of any city in the UK at the time and helped totally transform the image of Sheffield and its shopping experience.

Haydn Steers said: "City centre shopping in Sheffield in the seventies really was like no other period. It was a fabulous era and Atkinsons was undoubtedly the cornerstone of the retail experience."

Atkinsons produced their own commemorative newspaper to mark their 100th year and the face of John Atkinson fronted their promotions.

Over 400 bouquets of flowers were given away to customers; 100 'best buys' included crimplene coats at £8.50; "up to the minute styles" of hostess dresses at £4.25 and men's Evaprest trousers at £3.25.

On the entertainment and homeware front there was a Fidelity Stereo Musicmaster at £34.50; a Pifco iron for £2.90 and, to top things off, you could get a 13amp, British made plug for 9p (in the days when appliances arrived plugless and knowing your live from your earth was common currency).

Two years later and there was another pivotal date in the Atkinsons story - they announced a partnership with Sainsbury's which would transform their Moor store.

The Star reported at the time: "Sainsbury's, the London-based food group, are to open a 20,000 square foot supermarket in Sheffield.

"Work has already started on a £500,000-plus project in Charter Row, behind The Moor, which will include a direct link between Atkinsons family store and the new food market.

"A 450-space multi-storey car park is a feature of the development and Sainsbury's hope to open for business in the autumn of 1975."

Peter Atkinson, managing director of the store at the time, said: "The scheme was basically our idea and Sainsbury's were happy to take part in the project when we approached them."

He actually took the idea direct to Lord Sainsbury and arranged to meet him in London.

It was a very successful undertaking. Customers loved swapping between the two stores.

Patricia Eales said: "A trip to Atkinsons and Sainsbury meant you could get everything you needed in one go - it even had car parking. It was quite revolutionary at the time."

**Looking up a wet Moor
with Atkinsons on the left**

The store in the seventies

Peter Atkinson's 36-year tenure

Most shoppers remember Peter Atkinson looking most at home in his favourite department, household linens (in earlier years known as the "Manchester" department as most of the merchandise was brought over from there). In fact he regularly drove across the Pennines on "buying trips".

Once, when the local bakeries were on strike in Sheffield, he loaded his car up with bread in Manchester only to discover the industrial dispute was over when he arrived back at the store!

On another occasion he was on the verge of being stranded in Manchester by a heavy snowstorm but rather than stay there he managed to persuade a taxi driver to cross the Snake Pass. It ended up being the last vehicle to do so for several days, resulting in the taxi driver living at his home until the weather improved.

Peter originally helped resurrect the business after the Blitz with his brother John. But John's untimely death eight years after the opening of the new store in 1960 left Peter in charge for the next 36 years.

Peter had been involved with the business for over 50 years and had reached 80 years of age before he was persuaded to reduce his working week from five days to four!

The store's centenary celebrations

The Moor The Merrier after pedestrianisation

In more recent years the city centre has been vying for trade with Meadowhall.

At the start of the seventies The Moor was going head to head with the Fargate/Castle Square area situated just a few hundred yards away.

One journalist pointed to The Moor becoming "a withered arm" if drastic measures weren't taken.

Pedestrianisation was put forward as the answer.

Michael Holloway of the Sheffield Telegraph said at the time: "Most shoppers and traders on The Moor are in favour of Sheffield's second most important shopping area becoming a traffic-free precinct according to a survey which is so recent it hasn't been published yet.

"It's just as well they are. Something must be done to make The Moor considerably more attractive to shoppers if it is not, in the next five or ten years, to become a "withered arm" of the city's main shopping area."

Pedestrianisation initially spelled disaster for Moor traders; people stopped coming because of confusion over new bus routes and questions over where to park.

But Moor traders came up with their own solution - The Moor The Merrier campaign.

Nicholas Atkinson, John Atkinson's great grandson, played a pivotal part in the massive, weeklong drive to boost trade and get people frequenting the area once again.

The store also launched a new fashion department, Precinct One, offering high fashion at competitive prices.

The event was seen as a major success. The Moor was back in business

Work beginning on the pedestrianisation of The Moor

The Moor prior to pedestrianisation

Neville's lifetime of service

Atkinsons has built an enviable reputation as an employer that keeps hold of its staff.

But few stayed longer than Neville Sharman who first started in 1964 and only recently retired.

He was just 16 when he started and went on to become the recognised face of the store's popular Cookshop department.

He said: "When I started I did a lot in DIY and gardens when we had those departments.

"I still remember the Easter events with live animals for the children which would include goats and chickens. That went on until the late 1960s.

"I started in the Cookshop in mid-1970s. I used to go to Frankfurt with Mr Nicholas on buying trips."
Neville remembers the perks of working for the store. "All staff used to get turkeys at Christmas. It was a bit of shock to have to start buying them when I retired!"
Even his wife is part of the Atkinsons story. Neville said: "I met my wife at Redgates - I worked there first. Her dad was Father Christmas at Atkinsons - he won an award for being the best Father Christmas!"

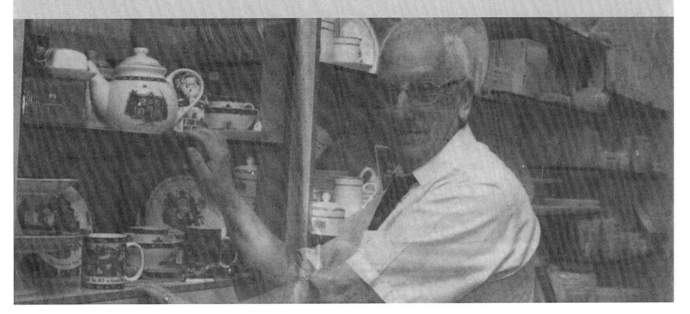

Neville Sharman

The city's Hole In The Road

100 Best Buys were highlighted in the 1970s

Luxury towels from the famous linens department, where 'Dorma' reigned supreme.

'K' shoes, a favourite for classic comfort

'Tricel' and 'Trevira' and 'Crimplene' fashions appeared for the first time.

Stetch Nylon suite and cushion covers made the sparks fly!

Clarks shoes, a byword for quality, then and now.

The latest double divan bed was just £36.50

As chairman of the Chamber of Trade, Peter Atkinson was instumental in obtaining Christmas illuminations from Regent Street in London

Looking up The Moor before the building of the Manpower Services building

CHAPTER TWELVE
The fluctuating fortunes of more recent years

No body blow has ever compared by the one dealt to Sheffield city centre by the opening of Meadowhall.

The unveiling of the sprawling retail outlet impacted on the fortunes of Moor retailers like never before.

Recessions came with the territory and you could normally see light at the end of the tunnel but Meadowhall was a different matter entirely, it was there to stay.

City centre shops were expected to drop 20% in turnover once Meadowhall opened. It was widely predicted The Moor would no longer exist five years down the line.

Nicholas Atkinson did an interview with BBC1's Look North programme to answer the dire predictions of academics from Sheffield University who said The Moor would not exist in five years time. He said: "We will wait and see!"

The rest is history as they say.

Meadowhall opened for business on September 4, 1990. It totally transformed the fortunes of the Lower Don Valley. It was hailed as "Europe's most exciting and ambitious shopping, entertainment and leisure mall".

The £200m shopping centre was timed to be open just before the World Student Games of 1991 - the latter becoming its own political bone of contention in subsequent years.

Sheffielders didn't need asking twice to take up the 12,000 free parking spaces. Meadowhall attracted nearly 20 million visitors in its first year.

The city centre became its poor cousin almost overnight and store closures soon followed.

Atkinsons, unlike many of its city centre counterparts, were well versed in coping with fluctuating fortunes and changes which were regularly out of their hands: everything from the pedestrianisation of The Moor (prior to it they'd have a readymade audience of queues of people waiting for the bus outside their store) to the end of the tram system a few years earlier.

They responded with what they do best, reinvestment

and reinvigoration.

The final stage of a £1 million investment was completed in May of 1992.

Lord Mayor Doris Askham cut the ribbon to open a new, £300,000 storefront which was the centrepiece of the works.

The occasion was marked by the addition of a traditional dance by a Chinese Lion.

Atkinsons had also added a new, self service restaurant, refurbished menswear department together with new concessions and more.

The investment wasn't an easy decision.

Graham Frith, then the store's marketing manager, said: "In a time of recession we had to decide whether to go ahead with the scheme. But the store has not been altered since 1960 when it was opened. That was 32 years ago and in retailing terms that is a long time."

Though Meadowhall was a massive threat to the city centre retailer, it did bring about one positive. Better relationships between traders, who needed strength in numbers to begin to fight back.

Graham Frith explained more of the reasoning behind the decision and said: "We see it as our contribution to The Moor Initiative. Retailers, the Chamber of Trade and Sheffield City Council have got together to give The Moor an identity of its own like Orchard Square has. Updating Atkinsons we see as part of an upgraded Moor area.

"It will mean our customers get even better service, with easier access to all departments."

One of the biggest sustained fight-backs by The Moor and partners came in October 1997 with the unveiling of a completely new look. The Star named it as "Sheffield's own Shopping Centre".

Around £2 million had been spent on the area's refurbishment and the great and the good had gone on record pledging their support.

The Moor now had new events areas; children's play area; better seating; lighting and 24 hour CCTV.

It also hailed the return of 'The Moor - The Merrier'

festival - the celebration first championed by Atkinsons a few years earlier that this year was offering fairground, live music and more.

But in many respects it was just cosmetics when you compare the £200 million that had built Meadowhall.

False dawns have followed false dawns but, however bad things got, Atkinsons still gave people a reason to make the pilgrimage down to the bottom of The Moor.

Prior to that, the early 1980s were not a good period for the Sheffield economy. Its heavy industrial base was in freefall as the steel industry put thousands of people on the dole.

The glitzy Fiesta cabaret club, which was thriving a few years earlier, had a weather-beaten 'for sale' sign outside it. The story was similar for many other entertainment venues.

Though unemployment was reaching record levels, Atkinsons was offering a dream start to working life for hundreds of the city's young people.

David McGuckin, like many, describes it as the best job he ever had.

He said: "I first started doing work experience there at the age of 14. I then went back at 15 at the start of a YTS programme. I remember it was quite daunting as we all had to turn up with our parents. It felt a bit like school. I chose to work in the loading bay as I'd already had experience there.

"Mrs Flynn was in charge of the loading bay, she scared everyone!

"It was the best job I ever had. It was such a friendly place. The YTS [Youth Training Scheme] might have only paid £25 a week but I made friends for life.

"I used to go and collect Mr Nicholas's son and take him to school - that was a real honour. There was always a great Christmas dinner and dance at Bramall Lane. I remember they sent us on an outward bound course to Cumbria once as well.

"I met lifelong friends, my first love and my first wife - all at Atkinsons!"

David McGuckin (centre) amongst Atkinsons cycling enthusiats in the mid-1980s after their journey to Skegness

In store in the 1980s

Blitz survivor Joyce Spurr with her painting of The Moor after the attacks

The 70th anniversary of the Sheffield Blitz in 2010 brought about renewed interest in the Atkinsons story. A commemorative plaque was unveiled and then, a few months later, a new book on the Blitz was launched from the store

Sheffield Blitz survivors Maurice Wilkinson (left) and Doug Lightning

Toasting the year 2000 in true Atkinsons style

There couldn't have been a more exciting way to enter the new Millennium than the store's £1 million expansion.

It was officially unveiled by the great, great grandchildren of founder John Atkinson;, Hannah and Rebecca Atkinson.

The extension almost doubled the size of the store and created 50 new jobs.

The move was prompted by Sainsbury's decision to move to a larger premises nearby.

It gave Atkinsons the opportunity to add new departments.

There had not not been a sizeable toy store in the city centre since the closure of Redgates and Hamleys a few years earlier and Atkinsons were determined to plug the gap.

The extension increased the square footage of the store by 24,000 feet.

Store manager Graham Frith said at the time: "The departure from the building of Sainsbury's gave us a fantastic opportunity to take a fresh look at our store and what we had to offer.

"Customers were consulted over what they would like to see in an expanded store and the result is a new toy department and the addition of children's wear, organic produce, sound/vision and electrical appliances departments."

The move was probably one of the smartest ever made by the store. The following few years saw a sharp decline in the whole Moor area. A situation exacerbated by the then soon-to-happen recession and the rise of on line shopping.

Indeed, Lisa Pilkington of The Estates Gazette, describing the area in 2010, said: "Empty stores and dilapidated and neglected properties on the side streets provide an unattractive environment for shoppers."

Many people were writing the area off altogether. It was a desperate situation with false dawns too many to mention.

Peter Atkinson celebrates 50 years of working at the store with his son Nicholas, business colleagues and friends

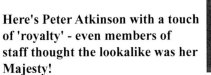

Here's Peter Atkinson with a touch of 'royalty' - even members of staff thought the lookalike was her Majesty!

Peter bows out in 2004 - but he insisted on business as usual

Peter Atkinson never really retired.

Despite being in his 80s, it was only in the last months of his life he was unable to take up his familiar position at the store.

"It was his life", said Atkinsons director Brian King at the time. "He was more or less full time right up to the start of his illness, about three months ago. He worked tirelessly for the company."

Though staff were out in force to pay their respects at the service, Peter Atkinson got his wish and it was business as usual at the store.

"The one thing Peter would not want is to inconvenience any customer", added Brian King.

Peter Atkinson started with the company in 1946 and worked tirelessly for it for the next 58 years.

The grandson of the store's originator, he was instrumental - along with his brother John - in ensuring Atkinsons returned to being a traditional department store following the opening of the present store in 1960.

Peter became chairman in 1968 after the death of John Atkinson and was determined to preserve the name of the firm as one of the foremost independent department stores in the city and the land.

It's fair to say he did that, and more...

Brian King said: "Throughout the difficult times he always kept us going and he'll continue to be an inspiration to us all."

Peter Atkinson actually started his working life in a store in London. As World War Two approached he was already a member of the Territorial Army.

When his call up came properly, the day before the formal declaration of war, it didn't go down well with his supervisor.

"Atkinson, you can't go to war on a Saturday!"

He ended up as the searchlight captain for a battery protecting London before serving overseas in East Africa.

There he spent several years manning artillery in anticipation of a Japanese attack.

During that time he also married a ward matron at the local hospital.

Back in Sheffield in later years he became a founder member of the Chamber of Trade.

His son, Nicholas, is now the face of the store.

He has been instrumental in bringing the business into the 21st century and has overseen new technology, new departments and the upgrading of the building.

The biggest challenge in 2000 was when Sainsbury's vacated their 24,000 square foot supermarket on the first floor to re-locate to a unit adjacent to the store.

This challenge was met with vigour and saw the creation of a much larger store that was able to introduce new departments and expand existing ones that had outgrown the original building.

Peter Atkinson celebrates his 80th birthday

CHAPTER THIRTEEN

The future could not be brighter for Atkinsons and The Moor

The whole Moor area is undergoing a much deserved, multi-million pound renaissance.

Developers are pointing to it becoming "the Oxford Street of Sheffield". It is The Moor's biggest redevelopment programme since it was rebuilt after the Blitz of 1940.

With the re-siting of Sheffield Markets, which already has footfall of 3 million a year, directly across the road from Atkinsons, the historic store looks forward to the prospect of better times ahead.

Moor retailers are gearing up to be at the heart of the city centre like never before. The markets are already being followed by Primark which is moving across town together with TJ Hughes.

Atkinsons had witnessed the sad decline of the whole Moor area in recent years. Footfall has dropped sharply over the past ten years. Many people have shunned it altogether in favour of Meadowhall or Fargate.

Though there have been few winners in the present recession, times have been especially hard for The Moor. The area was home to popular high street names like Woolworths that went into administration.

Many of Atkinsons neighbouring shops were boarded up and many wondered if there was ever going to be a way to stem the glut of negative stories virtually writing off the area.

But, like numerous times before over the decades, Atkinsons has somehow kept smiling; safe in the knowledge the values it has held since 1872 will shine through as the people of Sheffield continue to support it. It maintained its loyal customer base who carried on supporting the store regardless.

Finally, the tenacity and hard work by all concerned is being rewarded.

The route to regeneration has been by no means easy. The false dawns have been tortuous and numerous.

Come into Atkinsons today and you'll find a renewed air of confidence and a new look.

The store has invested over £350,000 on a totally new entrance; better lighting; first floor decor and more.

Atkinsons is also working hard to remind people of its position as Sheffield's only independent department store.

Nicholas Atkinson said: "Unlike the multiples, we're not dictated to by a head office in London. All our buyers live in Sheffield and know exactly what our customers want. Our region has its own particular style and taste and we've always tried to reflect that. Many bespoke suppliers simply are not big enough to supply national chains but they're perfect for us. It also means we're able to supply quality goods that are not available anywhere else.

Nicholas Atkinson, like Atkinsons tens of thousands of regular customers, thinks there'll never be a replacement for a good, honest independent retailer offering quality goods at the right price.

He said: "We are very aware of the rise of internet shopping and we are addressing this in our own way. However, we feel that we can offer the public of Sheffield something very special when they visit our store. We are becoming a niche retailer in a very cloned High Street and this will make us more popular in the future. With four restaurants and 36 departments we have something for everyone and of course we will make your visit very special and very different with our ability to look after our customer's every need."

The multi-million pound transformation of The Moor at a time of deep recession couldn't be more significant for the area. The renaissance is an obvious catalyst for Atkinsons commissioning this book.

Nicholas Atkinson said: "Both the store and The Moor have transformed many times since 1872 and it's an appropriate juncture to remind the Sheffield public of our unique longevity. It anchors our position in the city's history and gives "peace of mind" to customers, contrasting with the "here today, gone tomorrow" situation of some retailers and online sellers.

"There are several reasons Atkinsons has survived to be the only independent department store left in Sheffield. Our position at one end of Sheffield's shopping spine may have rendered the building and business less attractive for a takeover by one of the chain stores (a fate suffered by the likes of Walsh's, Cockaynes and Cole Brothers etc). The fact that all our merchandise buyers live in Sheffield so use their local knowledge to offer items that appeal to their fellow citizens. From the outset the Atkinson family have wanted to retain and grow the business for future generations to continue the tradition."

Nicholas Atkinson says, though the regeneration has been a long time coming, The Moor is finally going back to its roots of being the centre of the city: "Now that Primark has committed to its vast new store opening on The Moor in the autumn of 2015, many more retailers will follow, making the area a magnet to the shopping public of Sheffield."

The former Sainsburys store is now a bright spacious addition to the first floor

Fashions galore

Cook shop

Furniture department

The new Atkinsons entrance

Remodelled first floor fashions

A feast of fashion footwear

The busy coffee shop at The Moor entrance - one of four eateries to enjoy

The author

Neil Anderson's first introduction to Atkinsons was via the Muffin The Mule ride around 1970. It has been a constant for generations of the Anderson family - his grandma remembered the splendour of the festive window displays prior to the Blitz in 1940.

Being asked to research and write this book has been a true labour of love. The passion showed for the store by the public and former members of staff is truly infectious. Neil Anderson has compiled a number of popular books about Sheffield and its history. He has previously written for titles spanning The Independent to the Sheffield Telegraph.

Book cover: Ann Beedham
Book layout and design: Karen Davies
Scanning: Lowri Anderson
Proofing: Ian Cheetham and Peter Eales
Big thanks to all the former members of staff and members of the public that kindly came forward with their own memories of this great Sheffield shopping institution.

Peter Atkinson, the Grandson of John Atkinson, opens the £1 million extension to the store in September 2000 with the help of John's Great Great Grandaughters, Rebecca and Hannah.

The Charter Row side of the store, combined with the seven story car park dominates the entry into the city from the west.